THE GOLDEN BOY

A Doctor's Journey with Addiction

by **Grant Matheson**

The Acorn Press
Charlottetown
2017

ΛCⓈRNPRESS

P.O. Box 22024
Charlottetown, Prince Edward Island
C1A 9J2
acornpresscanada.com

Printed in Canada by Marquis
Edited by Ann Thurlow
Copy Edited by Laurie Brinklow
Cover and interior design by Matt Reid

Library and Archives Canada Cataloguing in Publication

Matheson, Grant, author
The golden boy / Grant Matheson.

Issued in print and electronic formats.
ISBN 978-1-927502-95-2 (softcover).--ISBN 978-1-927502-96-9 (HTML)

1. Matheson, Grant. 2. Matheson, Grant--Health and hygiene.
3. Physicians--Canada--Biography. 4. Drug addicts--Canada--Biography.
5. Physicians--Malpractice--Canada. 6. Recovering addicts--Canada--Biography.
I. Title.

R464.M354A3 2017   610.92   C2017-905361-2
                                          C2017-905362-0

Canada   Canada Council   Conseil des Arts
         for the Arts   du Canada

The publisher acknowledges the support of the Government of Canada
through the Canada Book Fund of the Department of Canadian Heritage
and the Canada Council for the Arts Block Grant Program.

The needle tears a hole,
The old familiar sting.
Try to kill it all away,
But I remember everything.

—from "Hurt" by Nine Inch Nails
(lyrics by Trent Reznor)

PREFACE

Montreal.
Victoria Day Weekend, 2005.

He sits in an airport waiting area full of happy travellers. Looks down at his dirty, rumpled jeans and wipes the sweat off his forehead. He restlessly taps his foot, making the black duffle bag on his lap bounce. Rolls his ticket between his fingers.

He unfolds the paper and checks the time. Looks at his gold watch and back at the ticket.

Running his hand through his hair, he looks again at his watch. Taps the rolled-up ticket on the duffle bag.

"This is a pre-boarding announcement for passengers of flight AC235 from Montreal to Toronto. We will commence general boarding shortly, but we invite parents of young children and those requiring extra boarding time to come now to the gate. General boarding will commence in five minutes."

Those around him gather their things, putting their paperbacks and newspapers in their carry-on bags. Zippers open and close as the travellers make their way to the gate. The soles of their shoes squeak on the floor.

But he stays seated.

Rubs his leg for reassurance that things are still in place, before slinging the duffle bag over his shoulder. He runs to the restroom.

Bursts through the bathroom door.

Walks past three men standing at the urinals and stands behind the man waiting for the only stall. "Can I please go ahead of you? I'm going to be sick."

When the stall door opens, he pushes past the man exiting it. His hands tremble, but he manages to pull the latch closed. Hangs the duffle bag on the hook on the back of the door.

Pulling down the zipper of his jeans, he feels his thigh for the tape holding the syringe in place. Holds his breath, rips the tape, grips the needle. Balancing the syringe between his teeth, he roots through his duffle bag past the snacks and books for the pill, the pill crusher, and the test tube.

Water.

He has no water.

Panic washes over him. Under the stall, he sees dozens of feet waiting to get into the toilet. Men are growing impatient.

The toilet is attached directly to the wall. No tank.

An announcement comes over the speaker...

"Attention passengers of Air Canada Flight AC235 from Montreal to Toronto, we are now ready for general boarding. Please come to the gate..."

His hands shake uncontrollably. A cold sweat breaks out on his body.

He dips the test tube into the toilet bowl, crushes the pill into a powder, puts the crusher back in his bag, and pulls out a lighter. Pours the powder into the tube of toilet water and holds the lighter beneath it. It bubbles loudly.

The people in line start to whisper.

He tugs at the upper sleeve of his shirt and pulls it tightly around his arm—a tourniquet. Pours the cooked Dilaudid into the syringe and looks for a vein. They are all collapsed but for one in his forearm.

He injects himself. His eyes close, and his mouth opens. His face instantly transforms from hard to soft as he enters a deep state of euphoria. Of ecstasy.

He pulls down his sleeve and gathers his things. He rushes past the men staring at him.

He gets to the gate just in time to catch his flight to rehab.

AUTHOR'S NOTE

It started with a cough.

As a family physician, I heard that line many times a day. A cough can be symptomatic of a chest infection or lung cancer, pneumonia or asthma. But rarely, as it happened with me, does an opiate addiction start with a cough.

I grew up in a religious household. One of three children (two boys and a girl), our father was a Presbyterian minister, and our mother stayed home to raise us. I tried my best to avoid disappointing my parents. I kept my nose clean and my grades up.

When I was eighteen, I made the decision to become a doctor. That's when I truly became the golden son.

I was serious about this calling to practice medicine, and I wanted to do whatever I could to help me along that path. I decided to take an advanced first-aid course, and I got my chauffeur's license so I could get a job working on an ambulance. I thought that would help prepare me for my chosen career. Every second weekend, while I was attending university, I worked from 5:30 p.m. on Friday until 8:30 a.m. on Monday.

I never saw anything as a doctor that scarred me like what I saw working on that ambulance.

While I was in university, I married my girlfriend. I was twenty-two years old. I remember walking down the aisle thinking, *what a terrible idea, you are too young to be doing this, what are you doing?* But I wanted to please my parents, and they thought I should be married.

Remember, I was the golden boy.

By the time I finished school and started practicing medicine in Montague, Prince Edward Island, my wife and I had two daughters, a beautiful home, and a picture-perfect life.

It came as a complete shock to everyone, including me, that soon after our divorce I became a drug addict.

Addiction stole a good portion of my thirties and also stole my career.

Many people have told me over the years that I should write a book. So that's what I'm doing.

Some details have been changed to protect those that I love, while still telling my story as accurately as I can.

I hope that everyone who reads this will understand both the overwhelming power of narcotics and that addiction can happen to anyone. Your kid isn't a bad kid because he or she is addicted to drugs. (And *you* aren't a bad person if you are addicted to drugs.) These people are into something serious and they can't get out of it. Narcotics are vicious, and they kill.

The man you read about in the preface, in case you haven't guessed yet, was me. You'll read more stories about him throughout this book. You'll notice that sometimes I write about him in the third person, and that's because he is now just a character to me. He is a completely different version of myself. He led to my destruction, until I helped him to get strong. And I never want to forget him.

This is my story...our story.

And it started with a cough.

Charlottetown, Prince Edward Island.
February 2000.

I sat on a leather sofa in an expensively decorated living room. I had a persistent cough, making it difficult to complete a full sentence. My friend pulled out two Cokes from the refrigerator and handed me one. I thanked him, took a drink, coughed again.

We were both in our mid-thirties. We ignored the hockey game on the big-screen TV, made small talk about the event we were going to: a dinner put on by a drug company. A chance for doctors to socialize and enjoy a free meal at the local Italian place. An opportunity for the pharmaceutical company to make connections.

I kept coughing.

"You're driving me crazy, Grant. Go take some cough syrup."

"I'm sure it will go away."

"You'll interrupt the presentation. Go take some."

I sighed. "Where is it?"

"Bathroom cabinet."

I dutifully went to the bathroom, opened the cabinet, found the bottle, twisted the cap, took a swig, and put it back.

We both finished our Cokes, put on our coats and went outside. We scraped snow and ice off the car windshield.

As soon as I sat in the passenger seat, I felt a warmth rise from my shoulders to my head. And the voice inside—the one that had been berating me day in and day out about my failed marriage—it faded away.

I was at peace.

After my marriage broke up, I had an extreme amount of guilt. As soon as I moved back to PEI after graduating from Dalhousie Medical School, I started building a practice in a small, rural community. It didn't take long until I had a full patient load. As soon as I woke up in the morning—every morning—this voice in my head would tell me I had failed. (Sometimes the voice actually came from my mother. Sometimes it still does.)

I'd failed my parents. I'd failed my wife. My church. My children.

I'd fallen in love with another woman while I was legally married, even though said marriage had been over long before I met the woman who would become my second wife. We'll call her Beth.

Even though Beth, whom I married in April of 2000, thirteen years after marrying my first wife, was truly the love of my life, I was living with a tremendous amount of guilt. I had traded the life I'd been living for a life I'd chosen. I was a terrible husband. Was I a decent father? I became somewhat of a disappointment as a son. My parents didn't even attend my second wedding.

This chatter went on inside my head constantly. I couldn't shut it off.

I was overwhelmed and depressed, but I didn't really think about how stressed I was until that night at my friend's house, when I took that cough syrup. My first step into that world of substance abuse was so innocent and it happened at the age of thirty-five. It was seductive, though; it made all of the guilt go away. The voices finally went silent. I felt such peace and calm. It was amazing, really. But, even then, I never sought out any kind of substance again. Not until about seven months later, September of that year, when I injured my ankle.

I'd been a marathon runner. And I had an injury that prevented me from running. The pain was bad, and I had a lot of stress in my life. I was missing that runner's high.

My daughters were four and six years old at the time, and Beth had just found out she was pregnant. I was working day in and day out, with a successful practice in Charlottetown. I was not only working my regular office hours, but I was also doing evening clinics and taking regular shifts at the hospital. The money was great. Much of it was going to my first wife for child support and alimony, but I was doing well as the primary breadwinner for my new marriage, and I was helping to support my parents as well.

But here I was with this injury. I couldn't mow the lawn. I couldn't run around the yard with my daughter on my shoulders like she wanted me to. I was in pain.

One day, a patient returned a bottle of Percocet to me,

to be disposed of. I thought I'd take half of one to see if it would make my ankle feel any better than it did with the Tylenol I had been taking.

And it did.

When the Percocet wore off, I took another one.

I was soon taking half a pill every few hours to keep the pain at bay. And I felt great. There was no shortage of Percocet in a medical clinic. Patients were leaving me with their unused medications all the time, and if I didn't have any, I just got more from the pharmacy. Beth was aware that I'd been taking this stuff, but neither of us was concerned. I was a doctor. I knew what I was doing. Besides, I was as straitlaced as they come. I would be the last person to ever develop a drug dependency.

I also enjoyed the extra rush of energy the pills were giving me. I had a hectic life. I was working through the week, picking up my daughters from their mother every Wednesday afternoon and every other weekend. While I had them, we packed in as many activities as we could. I was determined to play an active role in their lives.

The painkillers were not interfering with my life or my work, but they were certainly a constant. I had to have them in order to manage the pain, and to keep up with everything. As a doctor, I knew that the chronic pain in my ankle was worse because I was taking so many pain-killers. Looking back, I should have managed that pain in a different way, but I'd already gotten myself hooked.

As Beth's pregnancy progressed, we started making some plans to celebrate. We booked tickets to go to

Disney World together in the winter of 2001, to celebrate and to have fun as a family. I had a medical conference to attend in Orlando, so our accommodations would be covered. The timing seemed right. The girls were so excited! Both about the baby, and about seeing the "happiest place on earth."

But before Disney, Beth and I decided to book ourselves on a little getaway to Miami, to celebrate her birthday. I was making a lot of money during that time, and, boy oh boy, did I ever love spending it. I was on top of the world. Or so I thought.

One evening in Miami, Beth and I joined some friends for dinner in a great restaurant. I was on top of the world. I looked across the table into the face of my beautiful wife—the love of my life—and felt like I was the luckiest man in the world. She seemed especially beautiful there, in the candlelight, on the beach. Short sundress, long legs. Silky, dark hair.

Then, I could feel my buzz dying.

The bill came; I opened it. Dinner for two: $450 US. Unblinking, I set my credit card down on the table—nothing to it.

All the while the seductress was calling to me, like a siren would beckon a sailor into the sea. I needed to sneak away without raising alarm in my wife or our dining companions.

I was powerless. I loved everything about my drugs: the intoxicating scent, the thrill of possibly being caught with them, the way they made me forget about my problems and made me feel everything while feeling nothing.

I knew I shouldn't be thinking about getting high while I was out celebrating my wife's birthday. But I needed to.

Immediately.

I excused myself from the oceanside table and hurried

to the restroom. I walked through the gauzy white curtains floating on the ocean breeze. Reached into the pocket of my pants until I felt the pill. Put it in my mouth. Swallowed.

Release.

That happy buzz was back. I reached the restroom, basking in the sensation of stillness sweeping over every nerve in my body.

Then I had a moment, right in that bathroom stall. I was in this incredible restaurant right on the beach in Miami, with my beautiful wife, and I'd taken so much Percocet that my bladder couldn't relax enough for me to pee.

That should have been enough right then and there to make me seriously examine my behaviour, but I still wasn't ready to admit yet that I had a problem.

I was my own doctor, and I had things in check.

After we returned home from Miami, we were getting ready to take the kids to Orlando when Beth suffered a miscarriage. We lost the baby.

I was suddenly faced with this terrible dilemma. We were totally devastated by this loss. Yet, the girls were so excited to go to Disney World.

I had an impossible choice to make: leave my wife home alone after just having lost our baby or tell the five- and seven-year-old girls we couldn't go to Disney World after all.

We agonized over the decision and decided I would go with the girls.

I remember having that discussion with them. That the good news was: we were going to Florida. The bad news was: there would be no baby.

My life started to get much more stressful, though, during that solo trip to Florida. I had this conference I was there for, and so I had the girls in childcare at the hotel. I would blow off my meetings in the afternoon, so we could have our time together, exploring the Magic Kingdom and swimming in the hotel pool. I was taking half a tablet of Percocet every few hours, and I was feeling okay. I know now that drugs had distorted my sense of reality while I was down there. I was feeling like Super Dad for having my girls there with me on my own, but I failed to recognize the only reason I was able to cope was because of a chemical. With the Percocet, the pain was manageable—the physical pain and the mental anguish over leaving my wife at home. The Percocet helped to quiet the voices in my head, allowing me to get through the days. When I popped a Percocet, my ankle wasn't as sore, and my mind wasn't so busy berating me all the time.

I kept on taking them when I returned home. Every day. Multiple times a day. Again, I was able to justify my behaviour, because I was my own physician. Nothing to worry about. I was an excellent doctor.

Then, the following year, I attended a conference in Halifax. And it's there where I learned that I might have gotten myself into some trouble.

Halifax, Nova Scotia.
March 2002.

I was seated near the back of the banquet hall, waiting for the presenter to start speaking again. Dozens of doctors filled the rows of seats. I noticed there were fewer people there that afternoon, on the last day of the conference.

I looked down at the booklet on my lap: Health and Safety At Sea. Seafarer's Medical Certification.

I twisted the cap off a water bottle and swallowed the tablet I'd been keeping in my pocket.

The presenter changed the slide.

He flipped through the booklet to the corresponding slide:

Symptoms of Addiction

High tolerance to the drug

Must take drugs to avoid or relieve withdrawal symptoms (symptoms may include nausea, anxiety, restlessness, insomnia, depression)

I could no longer hear the speaker reading the items on the slide:

Loss of control over drug use (user wishes to stop using but feels powerless)

Life revolves over drug use

Fuck.

I could no longer hear the speaker.

Continued use despite knowing the danger

I could feel my face flush. How did I let this happen? This is me. I am a drug addict.

Okay, Grant. This is enough. I'm done. We are done.

And I was.

Until I wasn't.

I honestly thought I was in control of my drug use. I was a doctor, for crying out loud! I knew how much medication I needed. And then I saw my own symptoms in that presentation. I had an epiphany at that moment: I'd been justifying my drug use all along, saying I needed the pills to make my ankle feel better. But I was using the pills when I shouldn't have been. And, as a doctor, I knew that with my pain receptors bathed in these chemicals, I was just making my ankle more and more sore, screaming for the stuff.

I didn't take any more pills after that.

Withdrawal symptoms kicked in right away. It was uncomfortable but not severe. It mostly left me feeling really depressed, tired, and weighted down. It felt like there was a bear on my back and every movement I tried to make was just so heavy.

I got back home on Monday and called the lecturer. I didn't give him my name, and this was before Caller ID.

I needed to talk to someone.

I told him that I was a physician from the conference on the weekend and that some of the things he spoke about—addiction—he was talking about me. He said there usually is someone in the crowd that ends up calling him to talk for the very same reason. It made me feel a bit better to know that other doctors and nurses ended up in the same boat as me. He suggested I see someone, which was much easier said than done.

I had to be extremely careful about who I talked to. If I told my doctor about a problem with narcotics, he would have a legal obligation to report me and I could lose my license. And if he didn't report me, and the powers that be were to find out he knew about it, he could lose his license.

So later that week I spoke to the psychiatrist I'd been working with since my divorce. I couldn't tell him about the drugs, but I could talk about my depression. I was getting more depressed with the withdrawal, that was true.

I had taken that week off work because I had no energy and because I needed to right myself. I couldn't get off the couch. I was going through pretty standard withdrawal: nausea, diarrhea, hot and cold sweats.

Because I had to explain these symptoms without including the bit about drugs, my psychiatrist simply thought I was depressed. He actually suggested that I may be manic depressive. Perfectly sensible because I would have these highs (on drugs) and lows (not on drugs). I loved that I had this to tell people. Being manic depressive is way better than being a drug addict. I was prescribed Lithium, which did nothing for me, but I took it to make the College of Physicians happy.

I got through that week or ten days of discomfort (the withdrawal really wasn't all that horrible) and that was the end of that. I was doing well. By the time my birthday rolled around in April, life was good. I had been clean for a solid month but I was a little bit agitated. The best way to describe what I was feeling is that I was on edge for no good reason.

We were expecting another baby and we were thrilled about that, but I was feeling a bit unsettled. I gave up my hospital privileges at this time to alleviate some of the work pressure I was under, to see if that might ease the stress.

On Victoria Day weekend, we were attending a wedding in Lunenberg, Nova Scotia. We booked ourselves into a little bed and breakfast. When we arrived, we realized I had forgotten my suit.

Great. Here we were in a small town with nowhere to shop for a suit except a thrift store.

There was one suit there that fit me and it was like a Halloween costume. I felt like a mobster in this wide-collared pinstriped suit. It was ridiculous. It smelled weird. It was horrible.

I was sitting there, feeling awful, between a friend of mine who looked so good in his expensive suit and my gorgeous, perfectly dressed wife.

I didn't have that numbness from my painkillers, so I decided to drink away my feelings. I had never been a drinker. Here I was in my late thirties, and the most alcohol I had had was a couple of beers in a social setting. I didn't have much of a tolerance for alcohol. And I never really considered how alcohol might affect me since getting off the Percocet.

After a few glasses of Rose wine, I stopped caring about the suit. I stopped caring about anything. I finally had that sense of calm back. The same feeling I would get from my pills.

So I kept drinking.

Four glasses of wine turned into eight glasses of wine turned into nineteen glasses of wine turned into twenty-eight glasses of wine turned into thirty glasses of wine turned into a memory I wish I could forget.

Lunenburg, Nova Scotia.
May 18, 2002.

I lay on the bed in my socks and underwear, pieces of my suit strewn around the room. Beth, her rounded abdomen visible beneath her nightdress, tried to pull the white duvet out from under me.

"You're so beautiful," I slurred. "I think I drank a little too much."

"Jesus, Grant, get up!"

But she was too late.

I was heaving the contents of my stomach onto the duvet.

Beth kept me propped up on my side. "No, no, no, no!"

My body lurched and went limp. I wiped my mouth with my arm, "I think I need some water."

She passed me a glass of water. I took a sip. I set the cup on the bed, spilling the rest of the water. I found my way to my feet, lay on the couch at the opposite side of the room, and passed out.

"You bastard," she said. She folded the duvet and carried it to the bathroom where she tried to scrub it clean.

That drinking binge was the first time I ever did anything like that. I felt horrible. I was so drunk I couldn't clean myself up. It was completely out of character for me.

I know now that I was overcompensating, trying to get that same feeling I was missing from the pills. But it hadn't worked, and I was ashamed of my behaviour. So enough of that.

I spent the summer working as many hours as I could, without the hospital shifts. A lot of people were depending on my income: two daughters, an ex-wife, a current wife, aging parents, and a baby on the way. There was a huge financial strain on me. And, as a physician, it was always a catch-up game with Canada Revenue Agency, paying off taxes from the previous year. No wonder I was feeling agitated.

I took some time off work to be with my daughters before school started again. We were trying to pack in as much fun as we could. They were keeping me busy, and I was dearly missing my old friend, the one who kept me calm and gave me the energy to do all those fun things with the girls—and the ability to work a hundred or so hours per week with ease. I clearly recall spending a week of vacation at my in-laws' cottage thinking, *Okay. I just have to get through this week and get back to work into a regular rhythm and everything will be all right. Just get through this week.*

I was trying so hard to stay strong in my recovery. And I was doing well.

Knowing what I do now, that drinking binge indicated that I was in clear danger of relapsing, but I didn't know anything about addiction then.

In med school, we had to attend one AA meeting. That

was the extent of my addictions training. I knew nothing about addiction recovery. I hadn't even heard the word relapse before I went to rehab. I didn't know classic things about addicts, like bargaining, minimizing, and justifying. I didn't know anything about any of it.

Things are a little better now, but for the most part, medical schools were once notorious for teaching next to nothing about addiction. These are the people giving out narcotics, and yet they are taught nothing about the dangers of addiction.

I was doing a horrible job of being Grant's doctor. I was totally ill-equipped to help him. I didn't know how much trouble he was in. There were no second opinions to be had. So Grant kept on going without any support.

Until the last weekend in September when Grant's brother...my brother...walked into my office on a Monday morning in very rough shape. And then our world came crashing down.

He walked into my office wearing a plaid shirt, faded jeans, a leather motorcycle jacket, and well-worn Kodiak boots. He shut the door behind him.

I told him to take off his sunglasses.

He did. He put his sunglasses in the pocket of his leather jacket. His eyes were bloodshot, his pupils narrow. He sat down in the chair in front of my desk.

"Jesus, you're in rough shape. What happened?" I asked him.

"I don't know what to do," he said.

"Are Mom and Dad all right?"

He nodded. He put his face in his hands.

"I need you to give me a prescription. I'm in bad shape, Grant."

"A prescription for what?"

"Dilaudid."

"What? What have you gotten yourself into? I can't write you a prescription. Can't do it."

"Please, Grant." He was sweating, hands trembling. "I'm in bad shape."

"Go see your own doctor. I can't help you."

"He's on vacation, I have nowhere else to go."

"You're going to have to wait, Buddy. I can't help you. Go see my psychiatrist." I wrote down a name and address on a piece of paper and handed it to my brother.

He took the piece of paper. He looked down at it and back up at me.

"I'll go see him now. After that, I'm going home to drink. Can I drink?"

"Go ahead," I said. "Go home and drink. But I can't do anything for you."

So that's what he did. He got drunk.

On the final day of his life.

I'd always believed that my brother and I couldn't have been any different. And, yet, it seems that we were more alike than I ever could have imagined.

I had no idea he'd gotten himself hooked on Dilaudid. Yet, here he was in a bad case of withdrawal, looking for a prescription. I couldn't do what he was asking me to do. Especially not after what I'd just been through myself.

I thought about his visit all day long. I couldn't shake this feeling that something bad was going to happen.

That evening, Beth and I decided to have dinner outside. It was a beautiful autumn day... warmer than usual for the end of September. Beth was getting supper ready and I just couldn't shake this horrible feeling. I was pacing the deck thinking about my brother. I called his house but he wasn't home. I told his wife he wasn't in good shape earlier that day. I suggested she go out and look for him. She said she would.

A little while later I tried calling my brother again, but there was no answer. I figured his wife had gone out to the bars to find him, so I left it at that.

After dinner, Beth and I were on the couch watching television when the phone rang. And I got the worst news of my life.

It was my sister-in-law.

I couldn't make her out at first because she was crying.

I knew what she was going to tell me before I picked up the phone.

RCMP. Accident. Driving drunk.

Dead.

My brother was dead. And it was all my fault. It was all my fault.

My world stopped in that moment.

I remembered thinking that afternoon, what if he dies tonight? I should have followed my gut. I should have gotten in my car and driven to the bars until I found him. But I didn't.

Instead, here I was, having to drive to my parents' home and wake them with the news that their son had died. I was trying to console his wife. It was me who told my niece that her father was dead.

Apparently, he did try to get in to see the psychiatrist, but he was turned away. The receptionist gave him an appointment for the next day.

Dad and I both went to the morgue to identify the body. Because we had to.

The days that followed were a blur.

During the funeral mass, some bikers made an appearance to show their respect. Nobody had any idea that my brother was involved in a gang. Least of all our father, the minister.

The bikers were very respectful. They did a ceremony at the casket and they led the procession to the graveyard without their helmets.

I was in this daze. I had no idea who my brother was and I never will.

I knew something was going on, but he would deny using drugs anytime I brought it up. He'd gotten hurt the year before and was on prescription painkillers. Mom had said to me at one point that she was worried he was addicted to them, but I didn't want to hear about it. I was trying to do everything I could to not be part of that world.

I had to go back to work the day after the funeral, and I was putting everything I had into that. I was working to manage my stress. I always found solace in my work, especially evening clinics. I used to love those. I sincerely enjoyed being a physician, and I especially loved when I could see five or six patients in an evening clinic and I was presented with these puzzles to solve. I loved finding issues that were overlooked by other doctors. I was a good doctor and I loved helping people. So I focused on that.

I had an extremely difficult time coping with my brother's death. I didn't even want to face my psychiatrist. I was so angry with him for not seeing my brother that day. When I did go in to see him, he gave me a big hug and I distinctly recall wanting to punch him in the mouth. I couldn't open up to him now because I hated him. Never mind the fact that I was hiding the addiction I was trying to deal with.

He put me on antidepressants, but they weren't touching the pain. Not like my old friend, Percocet. But I wasn't going down that path again. My wife was about to give birth.

Two weeks after my brother died, I was completely overwhelmed. I made a decision that will haunt me for the rest of my life.

I paced the floor. My daughters giggled in their room across the hall. It was my weekend with them and they were waiting for me to play with them. I had forts to build, grass to cut, clinics to work. Beth could go into labour at any minute...

"You just have to get through this week," I told myself— the same line I'd been feeding myself since the funeral.

I sat on the bed, facing the antique cabinet. I heard a voice I hadn't heard in six months—the seductive voice of my former lover.

Something is wrong with the child your wife is carrying. You will have to pay for killing your brother. But don't worry, I will make the pain go away. I will make it all go away.

I put my head in my hand and rubbed my temples. I believe I could actually feel her and smell her. I wanted her, just once more.

I stood up, put my hand on the cabinet.

I crossed the room, found the key, returned to the cabinet, fingered the lock. I inserted the key.

Click.

The lock turned.

The door opened.

I could hear a voice.

"You just have to get through this week. You just need

to feel numb for a little while."

Among the pill bottles I found the one I had put there in case I needed it.

OxyContin (oxycodone hydrochloride extended-release tablets) 20mg

100 Tablets Rx Only! Keep out of reach of children.

I popped the child safety lock. Twisted open the bottle. Dropped one round white pill in my hand.

"If you do this, are you going to be able to stop?" I asked myself.

The voice of the Oxy soothed my worries. *It's just a low dose. You'll only need one and you'll feel so good all day long.*

I swallowed the pill. I put the bottle in the drawer, locked the cabinet. I felt immediate release wash over my entire body. I left the room, played with my kids, cut the grass, kissed my wife, survived the day.

After my brother died, I took a bottle of OxyContin home with me and added it to my stash of medications, in case I ever needed it. That will tell you how sick I was, but as a doctor, it was easy for me to justify that to myself. I kept all kinds of medications on hand, just in case.

OxyContin, we'd been told by the drug reps, wasn't an addictive drug, so it was a safer form of pain management. And because it was slow release, the pain sufferer would get all-day relief from a smaller dosage.

When I was in my bedroom that day, completely overwhelmed with life, I thought maybe it could help me. My ankle was bothering me again. I wasn't able to run anymore, I wasn't able to get to the gym. I was stressed to the max, and I needed to work more and more hours to pay for this money train I'd gotten myself on. I was on a financial hamster wheel I couldn't get off of. Maybe the pills in that bottle were the answer.

When I took the pill, I had immediate relief, but I felt like I was going to remain in control. The Oxy numbed me nicely from my worries while giving me the boost of energy I was looking for since I had stopped taking Percocet.

I was feeling good, so I was able to work even more hours than the hundred or so hours per week I'd been working. But I was setting myself up on a schedule that was impossible to maintain without chemicals.

I was overworked, I was under huge financial strain, I was mourning my brother's death for which I felt very much responsible, and I was about to welcome my third child into the world.

I couldn't talk to anyone about any of this, which created the ideal conditions for drugs to reenter my life.

I knew pretty quickly that I was starting to unravel, but I felt like I had no choice but to keep doing what I could to support my family. That meant giving in to the cravings.

Soon, I had no choice, anyway, because I was totally dependent. I wasn't using drugs for fun. I was using them so I could achieve everything I needed to achieve.

As a doctor, there was nowhere I could turn for help without fear of losing my license. And so I could see no way out. And so I kept on taking the pills.

Charlottetown, Prince Edward Island.
October 17, 2002.

Beth called me at the office. A few questions confirmed she was in labour. I tended to my last couple of patients, popped a pill, and headed home to get ready for the arrival of our new baby.

The fact that I went in to work the evening clinic while my wife was at home and in labour will give you some insight into where my head was during that time.

When I got home after leaving the clinic, I realized that I shouldn't have taken anything. I wanted to be on my game while this was happening. The love of my life was having our child and I would be present for this.

I was there with her throughout the labour, which lasted all through the night. I was completely sober the next morning when our daughter was born. The high I had when I looked into her face for the first time was a natural one. But within hours, I was high again.

Taking care of a newborn with my schedule was proving difficult. I was now not just the major breadwinner in our family... I was the only one bringing in an income. I still wasn't working shifts at the hospital, but I was working my regular office hours, and I was making good money doing evening clinics and clinical trials. I was going back and forth between OxyContin and Percocet in order to keep up with everything. And though I was, indeed, chemically dependent, nobody (aside from me) was concerned, because I was able to keep up with all of the demands that were on me, and I was bringing in about $300,000 per year.

I just had to keep up.

To make matters worse, that winter the dynamic at home changed. My marriage failed. The only way I was able to cope was with my friends, Oxy and Percy. The following spring I came upon a car accident that triggered a series of events that had a tremendous impact my life. Though I wasn't in the accident myself, it almost ended up killing me.

Charlottetown, Prince Edward Island.
May 2003.

He sees the crumpled car on the side of the road and instinctively brings his car to the soft shoulder of the highway.

His pace quickens, a surge of adrenaline speeds through his veins.

Pulls an Oxy from his pocket. Swallows.

Runs to the wreck. He hears sirens in the distance.

He notices her right away. She's thin with jet-black hair, performing chest compressions on a man. She's covered in blood.

"I'm a doctor," he tells her. "How can I help?"

"Under control," she says.

The ambulance is there now. One of the paramedics takes over for the woman.

He can't take his eyes off the woman. "We're both witnesses. We should exchange information," he tells her.

She pulls a pen out of her purse and reaches for his hand. Writes her phone number on the palm of his hand.

He feels sparks.

He takes the pen, starts to write his number on her palm. Notices marks on her forearm. *Trackmarks?* He is both unnerved and excited with the Oxy coursing through his veins.

And he knows he's in trouble.

Her name was Scarlett—the woman I met at the accident. I called her that same evening because I couldn't stop thinking about her. She was beautiful and dangerous. She reminded me of Beth.

I should have known better than to get involved with another user, but I was under the influence. Too far gone. It might have been the trackmarks that made her so attractive to me at the time.

I called her and asked her to dinner. She said yes.

The following day, I went to the pharmacy after work to see about putting together a proper roadside first aid kit. The accident made me think that, as a doctor, I really should have an adequate kit in my car, just in case.

I simply asked the pharmacist, "What should a doctor have in a proper roadside kit? Can you help me put one together?"

The pharmacy team put a kit together for me. It was pretty impressive, really. I had cardiac meds, epinephrine, a stitching kit, an intubation kit, and injectable pain meds. Not your average first aid kit. I put it in the car and didn't think anything else of it. Until a week or so later, after Scarlett and I had gone back to my place after our first date.

It was a little unusual, as first dates go. I sat across from her at the restaurant, sipping red wine. I noticed not her beauty, but the marks on her arms. I was both nervous and intrigued. She saw that I noticed, but she didn't hide them. She whispered, "Have you ever tried?"

I shook my head, no. Then she smiled at me and said, "You don't know what you're missing."

I asked her, "Which drug?"

"Demerol."

"What does it feel like?"

"It makes you feel warm all over. Like some blissed-out state of euphoria."

"I have some, you know."

"Some Demerol?"

I nodded. "I've never tried it before. I have vials of it in the car. In my first aid kit."

She grinned mischievously at me, almost a dare. "Do you want to try?"

"I want to try with you."

After dinner, we went back to my place. I carried the leather first aid bag in from the car. We sat on the couch, had some more wine. After a while she tied her hair back in a ponytail. I opened the bag. My heart was racing. I found two vials, two syringes.

"Have you tried anything before?" she asked me. "Are you sure you want to do this?"

I surprised myself by admitting I had taken Oxy.

"Well, it's hardly different than that. It's basically like smoking a joint, really."

I smiled at her and broke the top off the first vial.

"You do me first," she said coyly.

I drew the clean Demerol into the first syringe. Then the second.

I put my hand on her arm. "You ready?"

She looked into his eyes. "I am."

I injected the Demerol into her bicep and dropped the empty syringe on the coffee table. Then I took the other syringe and injected myself. I put the syringe down. We lay back, holding hands in a state of euphoria.

Even though I knew we were going down a dangerous path, I had justified it to myself. If I injected intramuscularly, I reasoned, it wouldn't really be that much different than taking oxy orally like I'd been doing.

When we did this, it really lowered the bar for me. I shot up drugs with this woman and it felt amazing and we got away with it. I had easy access, and I knew what to do. Within a couple of weeks, I went from shooting into the muscle to shooting into the vein.

Our relationship quickly intensified. That tends to happen when drug use becomes a couples activity.

Scarlett and I acted like bad kids together. We would experiment with anything. Whether it was coming upon a nude beach and dropping our clothes or injecting Demerol, there was little we couldn't convince each other to try.

We fell madly in love, and we had so much fun together...mind you, not always in the healthiest of ways.

My go-to drugs were still OxyContin and Percocet because a) I was hooked on them, and b) they gave me a pleasant numbness for twelve hours. They were still the culprits who held the most power over me.

I was also injecting Demerol and/or Dilaudid that summer, but only once in a while for that rush of euphoria I would get from it.

So there I was again at the point where I had to take a pill when I woke up in the morning, or I would be in withdrawal. I was never really stoned, except when I decided to inject Demerol, but I was walking around just as numb. Like any other person suffering chronic pain who is on opiates. You could only really tell by looking into my pupils that something wasn't right.

I was sick when I didn't take it. I wasn't taking it at this point to get rid of any feelings, because I had stopped being able to feel ages before. I was taking the narcotics at this point because I couldn't not take them.

At one point, I found myself stuck in traffic, late for work. I inched along. I called the office to tell them where I was. I checked the mirrors, turned the radio on and off. I was getting tense. Then, I reached into my pants pocket. I used my teeth to pull the shoulder of my shirt tight around my arm. One hand on the wheel, one on the needle, I injected Dilaudid into my vein.

Nerves stopped screaming. Light turned green.

By the summer of 2004, I was in serious trouble. I was now using intravenously on a regular basis, on top of the oral Oxy and Percocet use. Access was becoming a problem, because I was using so much. I was out of pills.

I'd started going around to all the pharmacies in the Charlottetown area and getting large quantities of

Dilaudid. It's ironic that Dilaudid became my drug of choice after what had happened to my brother, but I had gotten it in pill form one time and liked the way it made me feel, so it went from there.

The pharmacies kept giving me these vials of Dilaudid for office use. I knew I was going to get caught because a doctor going around from pharmacy to pharmacy for heavy-duty narcotics in a small town is going to raise a red flag. But I wasn't thinking clearly at this point. I was using intravenously every three hours around the clock.

That's how quickly it escalated. And it got uglier and uglier. Faster and faster.

Charlottetown, Prince Edward Island.
July 2004.

Scarlett had gone to the mall. I sat on the black leather couch, watching TV. Beside me were two vials of Demerol.

My daughter was playing in the next room.

I broke open a syringe, drew up the Demerol, injected myself.

I could feel pleasure rising from my toes to my ears.

Five minutes passed. I injected the second vial.

Within seconds, my body slumped down, my heart beat irregularly. Blackness fell over me. I felt like I was dying and I panicked. I managed to get my phone out of my pocket. I begged her to come home immediately.

My daughter had come into the room. I looked at her and all I could think was, *what did I do?*

I got a good scare then, the first time I accidentally overdosed. My daughter was playing by herself and here I was unable to get up off the couch. I kept thinking: *oh my God. I killed myself. I overdosed! What has happened to me?*

I honestly thought I was going to die.

That night, when my doctor (also one of my closest friends) showed up, he had no idea what was wrong with me. He thought maybe I was having a reaction to something. Of course I couldn't tell him what had really happened, so he was trying to do a diagnosis and was at a loss because he didn't have the facts.

And yes, I overdosed more than once.

Right after that the first time, I stocked up on Narcan and always had some in my drug chest at home. Narcan is an antidote used for opiate overdose so that I could accidentally overdose without having to worry about calling for help. Narcan blocks all of the receptors that an opiate lands on and brings them back to life.

The next time I overdosed, I was also at home. It would have been after that summer. I was sitting on the floor of my bedroom in a blissful state turned bad after giving myself too much Dilaudid. I had the Narcan in my sock drawer and injected a dose.

The problem with taking Narcan is that you end up in instant withdrawal.

Even though you've taken enough drugs to kill yourself, you want more right away after you've risen from the dead.

This was a good example of how I was blurring the line between being both a drug addict, and a drug addict's doctor. Instead of seeking help for the disease, I just stocked up on the antidote. The line had become so blurred that there really was no line at all.

Charlottetown, Prince Edward Island.
July 2004.

He spends the morning injecting Botox into people's faces.

He draws up the Botox for the next patient but his hands are shaking so much he knows he needs to inject himself with some narcotic to settle himself before he starts the case. Between appointments he rushes to the public restroom in the clinic with both syringes in tow.

Enters the stall. Reaches into his pocket for the cooked Dilaudid in the syringe. He knew he'd need it halfway through the day, otherwise he'd be too shaky to inject patients.

Makes a tourniquet with his sleeve, injects the needle into his vein.

Reaches into his other pocket, finds another syringe. His heart pounds. One syringe holds Dilaudid, the other Botox, the most poisonous neuro-blocker known to man. If he had injected the Botox, he'd have taken enough to kill the entire population of the world.

He falls to his knees on the floor of the stall. *I just killed myself*, he thinks. There's no time for an ambulance. And if there was, there's no saving him.

I'm going to be found dead in this stall with these needles, he thinks. They're going to think I committed suicide. Then his heart rate slows. And then he feels something else. Not death but the surge of Dilaudid starting in his toes. The withdrawal symptoms are gone.

He disposes of the needle and washes his hands. He goes back to work and hopes he has enough Dilaudid for the rest of the day.

Brudenell, Prince Edward Island.
August 2004.

I loaded a vial of Dilaudid into the last of the syringes. I carefully hid all but one in my golf bag. I checked my watch: 6:45 a.m. I wondered again why I ever agreed to this.

I pulled a dress shirt off the floor and smelled it before pulling it over my head. I stepped into a pair of khakis, grabbed cash off the dresser, and stuck it in my pocket, along with the other syringe.

I made the thirty-minute drive to the golf course, parked the car. I reached into my pocket and felt the syringe.

I bit the fabric from the shoulder of my shirt. I pulled it into a tourniquet with my teeth. I rolled up my cuff, injected myself, got out of the car, grabbed my golf bag from the trunk, and went to find the guys.

I felt great until the fifth hole. I was coming down, my score was going up. We didn't use a cart. At the sixth hole, the sweat was soaking through my shirt. I tried to stay cool in front of the doctors and lawyers I was playing with. But I couldn't concentrate; I needed to use.

I slipped a syringe in my pocket.

Then it was my shot. It occurred to me it would be easier to hit the ball if I saw only one of them. I looked down the green and saw I had a clear shot. I tried to focus. I swung and drove my ball as hard as I could into the woods. I went off to get it back. I found the ball. Then I made a tourniquet with my shirt.

I fed relief into my vein. Then I went back out of the woods and finished the round.

Though, on the surface, things appeared to be normal, there was no doubt that drugs were now controlling my life. That fall I had a chance to go to a medical conference in Paris. Scarlett and I decided to turn the trip into a holiday.

We explored Paris. At one point, we stood in silence, hand-in-hand, at the Alma Tunnel. We studied the messages written in graffiti for Princess Diana, there at the site of her fatal crash. The Eiffel Tower was in the distance, the golden Flame of Liberty behind us. Our arms were laden with shopping bags from Chanel and Louis Vuitton. I looked down at the traffic roaring through the tunnel. I thought about the crash that killed Diana. It occurred to me that, if I didn't get my life back on track, something like that could happen to me.

Scarlett's voice interrupted my thoughts.

"What time do we have to be back at the hotel?"

"Oh, I was thinking we could head back now, maybe drop this stuff off and rest before the dinner."

"Can we take the subway?" she asked.

"Really?"

"Yes, I really want to take the subway in Paris."

"Okay, let's go."

I was surprised that even here in the wealthy part of

the city there was a lingering scent of urine in the subway. Rats crawled around the tracks. I pulled the designer bags, and Scarlett, closer as waited for the train.

"It's what I imagined it would be," she said.

I laughed.

"Hey, do you have any more with you?" she whispered.

"Right here? Now? Do you want to find a bathroom first?"

"No, here is fine. Nobody is watching us."

I saw she was right. The men and women all walked by quickly, their heads down, trying to avoid making eye contact with the tourists and the riffraff.

We found a vacant bench, turned our backs to the commuters. I pulled the syringes from my pocket. I handed her one, kept the other for myself.

We both injected, then locked eyes in a spaced-out daze. We kissed, then stepped on to the train. The Canadian doctor and his lover on their way to a medical conference.

The conference was related to a clinical trial I was planning to be part of. I'd been supplementing my income for quite a long time by conducting clinical trials. I found them quite interesting, and I was offered many over the years because I had a very high participant retention rate.

But while I was in Paris I had this glimpse of myself, and how Scarlett and I must have looked to someone passing by us on the street. We were no different than a couple of street kids shooting up heroin. I knew I was in no shape to conduct a clinical trial and after giving it a lot of thought, I decided to give that up.

I was trying to offload some of my commitments to bring my workload down to a manageable level because even in the midst of the chaos and the sickness, I could feel myself spinning out of control.

My day-to-day was a blur. Scarlett was becoming an even heavier drug addict than I was. She was battling her own demons.

I was the functional one. I was getting up in the morning and getting my daughter ready for the day. But not until I took something.

I would typically wake up to my alarm around eight a.m. and my first thought was always about using. I was injecting throughout the day, in between patients, just trying to get through. When you abuse prescription drugs, especially intravenously, you learn that if you wait for your body's pain receptors to go into complete withdrawal, that sensation of using is amplified. I learned to wait just the right length of time so that I could enjoy that euphoric feeling because, besides that, drug use was not pleasurable.

It was a little over a year since I'd first injected and I was using about every four hours, around the clock. I would wake up through the night in withdrawal, and I would have to get up to use. I was a slave to the drug. I was getting huge quantities of Dilaudid from the pharmacies and I knew it was going to catch up with me.

And it did.

Charlottetown, Prince Edward Island.
December 2004.

I was on my way back from the bathroom where I had injected a vial of Dilaudid into my arm. My receptionist, who was also my mother, handed me a registered letter. It was from the College of Physicians and Surgeons. I went into my office and closed the door. I sat down at my desk and cleared some papers and a coffee cup out of the way. Then I tore the envelope open and began to read the letter inside.

...regrettably brought to our attention...no longer able to prescribe injectable narcotics...

That's all I could focus on, but that was enough. I put my head in my hands

Fuck.

I opened the letter and read it again.

...mandatory participation...pain clinic... Halifax...

They were on to me. Oh my God, they were on to me. Time was running out. What was I going to do?

My first thought wasn't that my career might soon be over. Or really even that I'd been caught in this huge lie. It was, "Oh no. How am I going to get more if they cut me off?"

I'd been reported by a pharmacist. Now, I was being ordered to attend a pain clinic in Halifax to "learn how to properly prescribe pain medication." I needed a lot more help than that, but that was my intervention: to go to Halifax and pretend I needed to know how to properly prescribe narcotics.

I saw this as an opportunity for me to paint a very nice picture of myself, so, in the days leading up to the clinic, I dropped my dose down as much as I could to function. And to compensate for the lack of drugs, I drank. Quite a bit.

I stayed with a friend of mine while I was in Halifax. It was the first time he'd ever seen me drinking. And we'd been good friends for a very long time. He had no idea about the drugs and he really couldn't have known even had I wanted to tell him, because he was a police officer. That weekend he was so incredibly annoyed with me. First, I drank all his liquor. Second, he was moving apartments and I was "helping" him move, though nobody actually wants a drunken fool to help them move. Besides wanting to kill me, he probably started to question what was going on with me because I would have been acting very much out of character.

I would drink in the evenings and go to this pain clinic with these specialists during the day, trying to look normal. I really didn't know what I was doing there. Surely the Pharmacy Board and the College...maybe even the Medical Society...would have had an inkling that I actually needed help, but their hands would have been tied without any evidence that I was the one taking the Dilaudid. They would have known something was going on, but until it was confirmed, there was nothing they could do.

It would be great to see a trigger system in place for health professionals in this type of scenario. Maybe a confrontation, a mandatory counselling session? I think I would have been ready at that time to just admit what was going on, and surrender to any help that was available. But who knows?

What I do know is that this was where things got very bad for me. Without access to my drug of choice, I had to come up with something else. I couldn't stop using. That wasn't an option. I had to work and pay the bills, and I couldn't do that if I was suffering through withdrawal. I'd tried that before. Didn't work for me.

The thing with addiction is that it plays off your strengths and uses them to get what it wants.

I was quickly able to learn how to crush pills and cook them myself, so that I no longer needed those vials of Dilaudid. I went to the pharmacy, bought a pill crusher and a lighter, and that's all I needed. I had all kinds of glass tubes and syringes at my disposal, and so I started making my own concoction to inject myself with leftover pills dropped off by patients. Taking pills orally wasn't enough anymore. It didn't give me the pleasure that injecting did. I had gotten myself into a very bad situation.

I got very secretive around this time, and I was again running out of pills. I was using so frequently that whatever was dropped off by patients was no longer enough to get me through. I was going to have to find a way to get more pills.

Sick Grant was functioning in his own vacuum, unaware of others. Like a toddler sitting in the corner, playing with his toys. Except these were not toys, and he was no toddler.

Charlottetown, Prince Edward Island.
January 2005.

He grips the cold metal bars. Scans the dimly lit hallway for a guard. But there is none. He hears a man crying. Another is whistling. One is screaming at them all to shut the fuck up.

The orange jumpsuit pools around his white sneakers. *How did I end up here?*

My heart pounded when I heard the mattress springs. I kept facing out between the bars, squeezing the bars harder. I bit down. I ground my teeth.

My cellmate came up behind me. He was a huge man, at least a hundred pounds heavier than me.

"I know you're a doctor," he said. I could hardly breathe. *Oh no, they know. How do they know?*

"You know the things you can do to make me feel good."

The man reached out to touch me. I closed my eyes, braced myself.

I woke up, drenched in sweat. I got out of bed to feed my addiction.

By the end of January 2005, I felt myself careening wildly out of control and I was afraid I was going to get myself into serious trouble.

Receiving the letter from the College scared me. I thought that the only way I was going to be able to stop going back to the pharmacies to get more drugs was to cut myself off. I contacted the College of Physicians and asked them to revoke my license to prescribe narcotics.

But coming on the end of February, I was regretting that decision because I'd run out of pills. Panic set in and I was willing to do just about anything to get more.

I was absolutely dependent on painkillers. I was a medical professional. A respected physician. A "pillar of the community." And I was a drug addict.

I know firsthand why people commit crimes to get drugs. For addicts, drugs are as important as air. More important than food. Drugs are everything. Addiction learns your strengths and uses them against you.

Would I have committed theft to get drugs? Probably. Would I have sold my body? I don't know. Maybe. But luckily I found a different way.

I firmly believe that the only way we are going to start putting an end to the drug problem we're facing in this society is to stop thinking about addicts as bad people. We are not bad people. We are sick people.

I was sick. And when I ran out of pills, I found a way to get them.

By breaking the law. I was a doctor, but I was a human being first. And I needed the drugs as much as I needed air.

He drops the coins in the woman's hand. She passes him a medium coffee with milk.

He nods a thank you, pulls down his ball cap, scours the dining room for his patient.

His supplier?

His dealer?

His...

"Dr. Matheson!"

Shit. He turns and smiles at the silver-haired man. Searches his mind for a name, but none comes. "Hello!" he says, distracted. He spots the man he's looking for, in leather, sitting in a booth facing the door. They make eye contact.

The old man makes small talk. Says he's feeling much better. "Glad to hear it," says the doctor.

"Well, I'll not keep you," the old man says with a wave.

"Take care," says the doctor on his way to the door.

He walks to his car, fumbles with his keys. Turns back to the coffee shop. Sees the biker heading his way.

He gives the man five brown bills for a hundred little pills.

Sits down in his car and drives home to cook the drugs

that he just bought from a patient. Wonders what his parents would think of their golden boy.

At first, I borrowed a few pills from a patient. I didn't really think much of it. I'd been complaining about my ankle when he was in my office, and he said he had some painkillers that might help, so I went with it. I didn't feel at the time that I was really crossing a line. But around that same time, I started buying pills from a different patient.

This patient had been getting narcotics from me for quite some time, but he'd had to start seeing someone else for the prescriptions after I was no longer able to prescribe them. I knew he was getting large amounts of pills, so I lied about this awful pain in my ankle and explained that it would save me a lot of hassle if I could buy some from him to save me from going to see a doctor myself. I offered him $5 per pill.

He thought about it for a minute and I could almost see the wheels turning, when he realized this would be a money-making opportunity for him. To sweeten the deal, I offered to buy a hundred pills.

It was a win-win situation at the time. I was getting what I needed, and he was earning good money. I was able to feed my habit—access was no longer a problem— but I was paranoid that I would get caught buying these pills. I knew I was doing something wrong and he caught on pretty quickly that he had me in a vulnerable position. I had nightmares about it all the time. I would wake up in a sweat: both drug-sick and terrified that I would get caught and go to prison.

It was in February that the College of Physicians started to request urine tests as a result of my being reported by the Pharmacy Board.

I was going to have to be creative to pass those tests because I was using around the clock. I thought I'd found a way when I decided to use a urinary catheter to put clean urine into my empty bladder. (Quite a party trick.) It didn't work. The test came back positive. So, they had to test me again, and I got a flag on my file.

My old friend Addiction helped me to get smarter, though. Next time I had a urine test, I was prepared. I put a tiny tube on a bulb syringe containing clean urine, and taped it to my leg. That worked. The test came back clean. They did more urine tests that spring and they came back clean, too. Because I was cheating.

During this time, I was being grilled on a pretty regular basis by the College of Physicians. I had to attend regular meetings in front of groups of health professionals to explain why I was needing all that Dilaudid. I just kept going with the same story, that I liked having it on hand for patients who couldn't afford it. Things were heating up, though, and I was starting to worry.

Scarlett was worried that I was going to get caught. Because, if I did, not only was her access gone, but our livelihood was gone, too.

I still had all my bills coming in, and I was working less. I had child support, income taxes, and regular expenses.

Never mind the cost of the pills. It was becoming almost impossible to make ends meet.

In March, I started thinking about getting clean again. I was trying to take fewer drugs, but to compensate, I was drinking more. And Scarlett was using pretty heavily at this point, too, which made it even more difficult to stop.

By now, my two older daughters, ten and twelve years old, were no longer wanting to spend time at my house. They could tell there was something wrong. And even though I wasn't drinking during the day, I drank heavily in the evening and I would get very foolish.

At one point, I'd tried to remain sober for one of those meetings with the College of Physicians. My lawyer gave me a look that told me I was in no shape to face this meeting. I knew I needed to go to the washroom and do what I had to do to make myself feel "normal" again. I had an hour of grilling ahead of me, so I could not be sweating and tremulous. I exited the restroom ready to confront the wolves. In actuality, they were the shepherds, but I couldn't see that at the time.

As badly as I wanted to get clean, I couldn't. I was too far gone. The jig was up.

In April, I received a letter in the mail, ordering me to fly to Ontario to Homewood Health Centre for an assessment, to see if I might belong there in their Addictions program for Health Care Professionals.

I took a week off work to try and clean myself up.

Charlottetown, Prince Edward Island.
April 2005.

Before I started, I made sure the girls would be with their mothers for the week, and then sequestered myself in the spare room. I knew that I would ruin our mattress if I tried to detox in our bed.

You need to keep in mind that I was not high, as you might imagine someone to be when they're injecting drugs every three hours. I hadn't actually been high for years. At this point, I was using just to stop the pain of addiction.

I knew what I was in for with this withdrawal racket because I'd tried to stop before. Quitting opiates cold turkey is almost impossible. A person really needs to be locked up and given support and medication to help manage the symptoms. I should have known better, but I didn't have any training in managing addictions. I was going to have to keep figuring this out on my own.

I learned I was okay until the six-hour mark, but then it would start.

The pain was unbearable...it almost feels like you're on fire.

Every nerve receptor in my body was screaming for me to inject something to make the pain stop.

I stared at the talking heads on the television, trying

to distract myself from the aching in my legs. I was wrapped in a blanket. My skin was a layer of goose bumps. I shivered while sweat dripped from my forehead.

My legs were crawling. If I'd had a bone saw, I would have cut them off to make the pain go away.

I refilled the glass on the bedside table: rum and ginger ale. I gulped it down. An urge ripped through my gut. I needed to get to the bathroom but I felt like I was moving under water.

Legs were crawling. I shook them back and forth but got no relief.

As I washed my trembling hands, a skeleton of a man looked at me from darkened eyes in the mirror. Yellow skin. Did I use a dirty needle? Could I have contracted Hepatitis?

My stomach turned. I threw up all the liquid I had drunk since the last time I vomited.

I rinsed my mouth, returned to the spare bedroom, legs crawling. I pulled the blankets around myself. I wanted to sleep but knew I'd have nightmares. I looked at the alarm clock on the bureau. The red numbers said 6:00 p.m., twelve hours since I last used. I drifted in and out of sleep, waking from nightmares. I was sweating, shaking, freezing.

The bedroom door opened and Scarlett came in.

"How are you doing?" she asked.

"I want to cut off my legs."

I drank rum straight from the bottle, then leaned over the bed and brought it back up into the bucket.

I wished I was dead.

Nonetheless, I drank the entire time I tried to get off the drugs. So much so that my skin was jaundiced from alcohol abuse. I was skin and bones. I had horrible diarrhea, I was vomiting, sweating, shaking, lethargic... exhausted. And the restlessness in my legs—they felt like my skin was crawling to remove itself from my body. It felt like there was a bear on my back and I just wanted to lie on the floor. I couldn't get up the stairs. Everything was so hard to do.

That seductress who made me feel so good when I would take a pill, years before? She was long gone. Now, Addiction wasn't sexy. She was a haggard old prison guard. I was a slave to this woman, and if I didn't use when she wanted me to, she would try to kill me.

An addict knows what it will take to make the pain stop and usually the drugs win.

My parents showed up at the house that week. They were worried about me because I rarely took any time away from work. They had no idea I was an addict. They wanted to take me to the hospital because I basically looked like I was dying.

I was completely out of it, but Scarlett wouldn't let them take me. She needed me to get clean because our livelihood and her access were in jeopardy. If I went to the hospital, the doctors were going to know what was happening and it would all be over.

I don't remember how she got my parents out of there, but she did.

I was terrified at the time that I'd contracted Hepatitis. I was diagnosing myself without really considering my full medical history. It seemed more likely to me that I may have used a dirty needle by accident, than that I'd drunk so much over the past few weeks that I was turning myself yellow.

At the three-day mark, I quit detoxing. I had to go back to work. I had to take a little something and then I would be okay.

I knew I was caught. I was being sent to Homewood for an assessment. I knew I was done, but I still couldn't stop. I injected myself. Immediately, relief came. From my toes right up to my head, through every nerve in my body. I felt so happy—so good. The misery was over. But then I realized I would have to go through the worst part of the withdrawal process all over again. Next time. But for then I had to get through the day.

I had to work. I still had the bills. I had to juggle work and the kids. And I was doing a horrible job. Still I continued to use, though in much smaller amounts, convincing myself everything I was doing was justified.

Since I failed in my attempts to quit, I had a new plan. I would wean myself down to almost nothing, and I would go to this assessment and fleece the doctors. This whole thing would be dropped. It was only 48 hours. I could do it. But for now, I had a birthday to mark. My brother was 41 when he died. I would hope I would make my 41st but I knew this all might be coming to an end. Hopefully not with flowers and a casket.

To celebrate my 40th birthday, Scarlett and I went to Halifax for the weekend. We had, I thought, an amazing time. We stayed at the Prince George Hotel. We got a suite, so the room was opulent. The shower was an open concept and could be viewed from the master bedroom. I watched as Scarlett showered and lathered her long lean body in soap and shampoo. For a minute, I felt guilty about dragging this woman along on my nefarious journey, but this was interrupted by her leaving the shower and dropping her towel.

"Why the long face on the birthday boy? I have a couple of things here that will cheer you up." The couple of things included sex and drugs, and then we were off to the casino. The Prince George is connected to the mall and casino by a series of pedways. Scarlett was wearing a tight short black dress with no underwear and high-heeled boots. The sound of her heels in the halls echoed through my body and made me feel invigorated. I love to walk when I am drunk or high, but even more so with an attractive woman on my arm.

We entered the mall area and I sensed the smell of new fabric, cooked food, and perspiration. We glided through the atrium oblivious to the other patron's scramble for last-minute purchases. We boarded an escalator to the pedway that would eventually take us to the casino. I went ahead, to help Scarlett exit the escalator, but not to be outdone she flipped her heels onto the mobile handrails. It was like a long sleek linebacker coming at me, except instead of a grimace I was distracted by a better view. She hit me hard and we both fell with a thud. I knew at the time we would feel it the next day, but a stop at the portable photo booth in the mall, and an injection for both, quelled any chances of us feeling it that night.

The Tuesday after Mother's Day, I was on a plane to Guelph for my two-day assessment. Scarlett knew what I was going for, but I hid it from everyone else.

I didn't think I would be going any further than the assessment because I was confident I would fool these doctors. I thought I was pretty clever. The night before, I went out into my back yard and scraped up my arms on the rose bushes, to cover the track marks in my arms. I've since wondered what the neighbours would have thought if they'd seen me wrestling with the thorny branches. I really believed I would be able to make this team of specialized doctors think I didn't have a problem.

Once the plane landed in Toronto, I got a rental car and drove myself to the B&B.

I dropped off my bags in my room, and headed to "The Homewood," as the locals call it. I was ready to breeze through the assessment and go back home, putting an end to this nightmare.

The assessment started with a physical exam and then there were all kinds of questions that I answered in the way I figured would flag me as not having a problem.

Do you drink or use drugs in the morning? Me: no. (But I did, all the time.)

Do you hide your drinking or drug use? Me: no. (But I did, all the time.)

Is your drinking or drug use affecting your work or family life? Me: no. (But it was, all the time.)

That was pretty much it for the first day. I got in my car and went to the liquor store. I knew I would have to be drunk to get through the next day of assessments. I went back to my room, got drunk, cooked some drugs, and injected them into my forearm.

The next morning, I had some more wine and some drugs for breakfast. After I injected, I walked to Homewood for my second and final day of the assessment.

The first half of the day wasn't much different than the day before. But after lunch, things changed.

I was meeting with a physiotherapist, going over exercises I could do to judge my balance, and there was a knock on the door. I was getting antsy. I wanted to go back to my room and inject again. I was surprised when the person at the door said Dr. Cunningham wanted to see me.

I didn't know who this doctor was, but my blood ran cold.

I was escorted to Dr. Cunningham's office. He wasn't alone in there. There were about ten people sitting in the room with him. Nurses, addictions doctors...everyone who had seen me over the past couple of days was there.

"We got a call from the Bed and Breakfast you're staying at, Grant," the doctor said, in his Scottish brogue.

I felt like a cornered animal. Someone had been in my room? My cheeks turned red.

"They found drugs and alcohol," the doctor said.

I looked him straight in the face and said, "It wasn't mine! It was there when I arrived."

"I can't believe you're trying to deny this," he said. "It's like you're standing over a dead body with the murder weapon. I don't believe a word of the shit coming out of your mouth."

I didn't say anything for a minute, and then I completely broke down. "You're right," I said. "I've been taking drugs every three hours for months. I'm drunk all the time. I've tried to stop but I can't..."

I spilled my guts to the people in that room. I told the entire truth.

After I was done, the doctor said, "You must feel like someone who has been juggling plates for years and you finally let them fall."

I started to cry then. "I don't know what to do."

"You're a sick man, Grant. Not a bad man. You need help. I would admit you today if I could but we don't have a bed. We're going to have someone go back to your room and remove all that stuff, and we're going to send you home. But you have to go to AA meetings and NA meetings until you come back. Do whatever you can to not use before then. I hope we see you again."

He said this, because the time before an addict goes to rehab is the most likely time they will die. The doctor was afraid I would overdose, trying to get one last high before rehab.

Two addictions workers went back to the B&B with me. I was embarrassed, but I felt like it was going to be okay. They moved everything around and tested it all to see what was in it. They were checking to see if the urine tests matched up.

I called Scarlett and told her to have something ready for me to inject when I got home because I was going to be sick.

When I got home, I really wanted to follow the doctor's advice to stop using, but I couldn't. Addiction had taken over my body and my mind and I just wasn't strong enough to overpower her. I was, though, smart enough to call my best friend to tell him what was going on: the Halifax cop, Donnie Buell. He had been my friend since grade seven, and over the years has become my best friend. He had this ability to allow me to show my fragile side. Perhaps it was his vast experience working with irrational behavior. Society itself seems to embrace the absurd. But when it comes to our own pod of existence, it is not so entertaining. I just wish more people were like Donnie.

Of course, he already knew. He'd noticed I'd been drinking, but he never in a million years would have dreamed I was also using drugs. I remember him saying to me, "I knew something was up when you were wearing long-sleeved shirts when we were golfing." I'd also been wearing a blue band around my arm for "tennis elbow" to cover my track marks.

He came from Nova Scotia to Prince Edward Island to stay with me the weekend before I went back to rehab, to make sure I didn't overdose. We both knew that the last days before going to rehab are the most dangerous for an addict. I didn't want to die from that last big "hurrah."

I made some calls before I left. Told my exes and my parents that I was going to be gone for a few weeks. It wasn't easy to find the words.

Beth wasn't surprised, of course. My first wife was shocked. And my parents? I don't think they could actually believe what was happening.

That their golden boy was a drug addict. He was going to rehab.

When I kissed Scarlett good-bye, we both knew that things would never be the same between us.

Montreal.
Victoria Day Weekend, 2005.

This is where it happened. This is where I was so desperate that I pushed past the men lined up for the bathroom
stall, where I used water from the toilet to mix up my
hit. I was on my way to rehab but I couldn't think about
that. I couldn't even face the short flight from Montreal
to Toronto without sticking something in my veins.

I started drinking on the plane. Even when I didn't
drink, I drank on airplanes.

When I got to Toronto I got a cheap rental car at the
airport. It was a little Toyota Corolla. There was a time
when I would have gotten the most expensive option,
but at this point, I was flat broke. Like most drug addicts
end up.

I had $600 in my bank account after I got the rental
car. I probably shouldn't have been driving because
I'd had so much to drink on the flight, but I probably
shouldn't have done a lot of things in those lost years.

It wasn't until I was almost in Hamilton that I realized
I was driving in the wrong direction. Before I turned
around to head to Guelph, I stopped the car and asked
myself if I really wanted to go to Homewood, or if I should
just say screw it and go to Toronto and party.

Reality kicked in and I asked myself how long $600

was going to last me. If I had $10,000 in my account? I probably would have gone to Toronto instead. But that wasn't an option now. I turned around and drove to Guelph. I dropped the car off at a rental place and hopped in a taxi.

"Where to?" the driver asked.

"Homewood," I said.

He looked at me in a way that I'll never forget. I wasn't the first person he'd driven to rehab. It was the first moment I experienced where someone looked at me as if I was a junkie. He wasn't unkind, but he was guarded. He didn't know me as the golden boy. As the doctor, husband, father, or the son of a minister. He just knew if I was going to Homewood. He knew I was an addict.

"I know people who've gone there," he told me as he drove. "They've done well. You'll do well."

I wondered what he would have done if I asked him to take me to a bar. But I don't think he would have. He encouraged me through his small talk on the ten-minute taxi ride. He really helped to calm me and made me feel like things would be all right.

When we got to Homewood, he wished me luck, I paid the fare, and hauled my ugly old suitcase out of the car and made my way to the front door of this imposing structure.

Homewood is an old redbrick sanatorium, surrounded by gardens and beautifully manicured lawns. At the time I wasn't seeing it that way, though. To me, in that moment, it seemed very much like a prison.

I struggled to make my way up the brick steps. I didn't know if I wanted to go through with this. But at the time, I didn't seem to have many options. I had no money, and everyone at home now knew what I was doing here.

I took a deep breath and went through the first set of doors.

The smell of hand sanitizer hit me. It was a familiar smell. Like the hospital. The SARS outbreak had just happened and there was sanitizer everywhere.

I put some on my hands and went through the glass door and whispered under my breath, "I surrender."

Guelph, Ontario.
May 2005.

He sits in reception, waiting for someone to take him to admitting. His hands are trembling. Sweat beads on his forehead.

How many hours has it been since he used? In the airport. Hours ago.

He looks over and sees a rough-looking man holding a black garbage bag. "First day?" he asks.

He nods.

"Me, too," the man says. "But I've been here before." He kicks the garbage bag. "This is all I have left."

He studies the man with the garbage bag. Pities him. Fears him. What kind of people am I going to be in here with? I'm going to be in here with...drug addicts like him.

Finally, someone came to bring him to admitting. He is examined. Is given an identification bracelet and his first dose of methadone.

Being in the position of patient was surreal. Between that and the withdrawal, I was feeling pretty antsy sitting at admitting. I had my vitals taken, and the nurse put a purple hospital bracelet on my wrist.

A volunteer walked me to my unit. As we went up a set of stairs, I saw a simple plaque above a door that read:

"Trust the process." I made a mental note to follow that advice.

The man walking me to my room tried to make small talk, but I wasn't really in the mood for chatting. Finally, we reached my room. My roommate was there. Lorenzo was his name. He left when we got there.

I laid on my bed while the volunteer searched my suitcase.

A nurse and doctor team came along shortly thereafter. The doctor asked me questions while the nurse took notes.

"What have you been taking?" the doctor asked me.

As a physician, you learn to protect the confidentiality of your patients. I had been acting as my own doctor for so long, I didn't want to tell him the truth. But I knew I had to be honest with him so I would get the appropriate dose of methadone. And I trusted him because he'd been through the same thing as me.

"80mg of Dilaudid per day."

It was the first time I ever said that out loud. But I didn't feel shame. I felt safe. Like I was protected. After years of trying to manage my illness myself, while caring for my patients, my children, I was ready now to let someone take care of me for a change.

The nurse administered the methadone and they left me alone to rest for a little while.

A couple hours later, I was nudged awake by my roommate. "Sorry, man, I know you want to sleep, but we have to go bowling."

I was disoriented. "Bowling? What?"

The methadone must be kicking in, I realized. I felt a bit better, but my bed was soaked with sweat.

"Yes, bowling." Lorenzo said.

I later learned that the rec team assigns each new patient to an activity when they are first admitted. I was in bad shape so I couldn't do anything too vigorous like basketball or volleyball.

It was late afternoon. After I was through at admitting, I really just wanted to sleep. The methadone helped ease the pain a bit, but I was drug-sick and I wanted to go to bed.

Lorenzo led me down to the bowling lanes in the basement of the building. I was standing there thinking, "This morning I was shooting up in the airport and now I'm bowling with a bunch of sober people."

I thought it was ridiculous. I wanted to use or to sleep. Anything but bowling.

That's not how things work at rehab, though. The program at Homewood is as effective as it is because it is so structured. It was go bowling, or go home.

There were about ten of us bowling. I started a conversation with a guy who seemed to be in worse shape than me.

After bowling, I went back to my room and lay down on my single bed. I didn't want to eat—I didn't want to do anything except be miserable. I wanted to call my kids, but I couldn't. Not yet.

The main doors auto-locked at 11 p.m. with a big bang,

a sound like you would hear in a prison movie. The doors were locked until 6 a.m.

I learned that night that my roommate slept in the nude. I also learned that he frequently woke himself up farting.

I had a hard time falling asleep. Sometime around 2 in the morning, I wandered out into the hallway to the nurses' station. I asked if I could have something to sleep. I was offered a cup of warm milk. I should have known better than to think I would be given a sleeping pill. Eventually I did fall asleep.

And that was the last day I would ever put drugs in my body.

The next morning I opened my eyes at 5:30. I tried to sleep some more but I couldn't. I heard the doors unlock with a big bang at 6, I realized I was drenched in sweat. I made my way to the shower.

In the shower, I looked down at my wrists as if I was seeing them for the first time. There were scars everywhere. "How did I cut myself?" I wondered." Did I make all these?"

When I finished washing the night off, I stood at the sink, looking at my gaunt reflection. My skin was yellow. I didn't recognize myself.

I left the shower and drank the first coffee that I could remember as a sober man.

I still felt like shit, but the methadone was taking the edge off so that I could function. That's why methadone clinics are so important. Methadone is a drug, but when prescribed by a physician, it eases the symptoms of withdrawal. I was on a tapered methadone program for my first week at Homewood, and it made all the difference in the world.

It was bizarre to start seeing myself through sober eyes. I was a complete and utter mess. I didn't look any different than that guy with the garbage bag filled with his belongings. He was probably looking at me the day before thinking the same thing I was thinking about him.

I couldn't believe the scars and track marks all over my arms. And I was so thin I actually shocked myself.

My sneakers were so disgustingly rank I had to throw them away. I didn't notice before, because my senses were all numb. And all I had packed were long-sleeved shirts and jeans. Guelph was experiencing a heat wave. I had nothing to wear. I remember laughing because that guy with the garbage bag probably had more than I did.

The routine I would learn on my first day was the same each and every day at Homewood. At 6:45 a.m., everyone met for morning exercise in the gymnasium. Whether you've been there for a day or a month, you're expected to be there for morning exercise. If you're late, you get written up. Everyone stands in a circle; homeless people, wealthy people, doctors, uber rich business owners, housewives, nurses...everyone's equal. After the morning stretches, we'd go outside for a walk around the grounds.

On that first day, I couldn't believe how green the grass was. I was in complete awe that there were leaves on the trees. That there was a smell to the outdoors. It wasn't all a blur. I was waking up! This is what the world looks like! This is what a bird sounds like!

I'd been numb for years.

This is why I was able to work as a physician while I was using. Opiates sharpen your focus on the task at hand. You're like a robot. You do this one thing and you don't notice anything else. The drug is all you need.

After our time outside came group. (Everyone is assigned to a physician and put into a group when they
first get to Homewood.) My physician was a big over-
weight guy. "What the hell is this guy going to do for
me?" I thought. But, it turned out, he was an addictions
specialist and he was in recovery. I learned that most of
the doctors there were.

There was a whole crew of professionals assigned to
our group: a doctor, nurses, occupational therapist, physiotherapist, addictions counsellor...an entire team.

During my first group meeting, when it was my turn to
introduce myself, the words were so strange to hear
coming out of my mouth:

"I'm Grant. I'm an alcoholic and an addict. My dry date
is May 23, 2005."

28 DAYS (PLUS TWO)

As part of my therapy, I was instructed to keep a journal.

This is a collection of my thoughts during rehab.

Day One.
Tuesday, May 24, 2005.

I don't see how writing in this journal is going to help me with my recovery but I am trying to keep an open mind. I did, in all fairness, fail miserably tending to my own care. They've made it very clear to me here that I am a patient and my medical degree means nothing. I guess I would agree with that. But it's hard to be a patient. I still can't believe it when I look down and see my name on my purple identification bracelet listed as the patient instead of the doctor.

The meds must be working. My withdrawal symptoms are manageable.

It was 1:00 p.m. when I registered yesterday. I spent the rest of the day getting to know the layout of this big old building and the program's many rules (exercise at 6:45 a.m., doors locked 11 p.m.–6 a.m., lights out at 11:30 p.m., absolutely no romantic relationships, etc.). There is still a voice inside screaming for me to run, and even though I have surrendered to the process, another voice keeps saying that when I get out I will try it again. Just once more.

I talked with others today who've been here longer. I learned they felt those feelings initially, too. I feel so much less alone here. There is definitely something to be said for being in a place where others are sharing the same experiences. It just makes it so much more tolerable knowing that I'm not all alone. I keep thinking back to my running days and how a marathon would have been so much more difficult without the company of others. My addiction made me feel completely isolated, even in a room full of people. But for the first time in a long time, I feel like I'm part of...something. Even though I'm overdressed in wrinkled, blood-splattered clothes from poking my veins repeatedly, and wearing a bright purple hospital bracelet on my track-marked wrist, I feel like I belong somewhere. And where I belong is right here, right now, sitting on this bed, clicking the night light off to end my first day at rehab.

Goodnight, Moon.

Day Two. Wednesday, May 25, 2005.

Today was my first full day of the program. The new admissions/patients are all filtered into one group that's called Phase 1. It's basically an educational week that looks at topics such as addiction as a disease, the addicted brain, impact of addiction on others, and how to participate properly in recovery groups. (Things doctors should learn in medical school, maybe. Just maybe.)

I'll enter a recovery group soon. We all will. And we have to be respectful, confidential, and, in the end, healing.

I'm still having a lot of physical symptoms. The diarrhea is interfering with my punctuality. We're expected to be on time for every session. Running to the bathroom constantly makes this difficult. I'm sweating, as Lorenzo likes to say, "like a whore at confession."

I didn't pack any shorts or T-shirts, which doesn't help. The nurses are saying the sweat is the drugs leaving my body. I think it might be the heat wave but true or not, that makes me feel better.

Other things that make this better:

This concept of "one day at a time" they keep telling me is the best way to think right now is giving me comfort

The thought of never using again in my life

The thought of just making it

Withdrawal is more manageable when you break it up into small portions of time. This helps me to stay in this day and not focus on how much I lost or would lose. I just focus on making it through this one day without using.

I have to force myself not to think of home. When I think of home, I start to cry. Not just a few tears, but blubbering sobs that activate my whole body into a convulsive shaking collapse. I can't go there in my mind. Besides, I'm supposed to be focusing on myself now.

My thoughts are seeming more rational now.

I go to bed tonight with the Seductress still calling, but she's not as loud.

I try to tell myself I will never use again, but I don't know yet.

Goodnight, Grant.

Day Three.
Thursday, May 26, 2005.

I'm waking most mornings at 4:30. Lorenzo throws his bed covers off during the night and lays there naked beside me on his hospital-style bed. Note: the beds are too close for my liking.

I thought about using today. I'd like to get a vial of Dilaudid. My symptoms are getting better, but I miss the routine. I miss it. I miss Scarlett.

My handwriting in this journal is even worse than you would expect from a doctor. My hands are shaking so much I can barely use them. I'm also getting worried that my brain is injured. I'm getting this odd, high-pitched noise in my head intermittently. It's like the sound of high tension wires in the summertime. I've stopped asking the nurses and others about my symptoms. I've come to realize that narcotics can cause a multitude of sensations, so of course I'll experience the same array as they leave my body.

I attended a Narcotics Anonymous meeting last night. I had no idea such a group existed and that there were regular meetings back home. It was like the AA meeting I went to the night before, but there were some differences. The one thing both meetings emphasized was that they were "we" programs. Recovery was an individual journey but the people who stay sober draw their strength from others.

I can't believe how many health professionals are in here. I thought I was the only doctor in Canada with a problem like mine. But I am not alone. It makes me feel better.

There was a rough-looking kid in the group. He looked like the classic idea we all have of a homeless drug addict. He looked at me and said, "Man, finally someone whose arms are worse than mine!" That was hard to hear.

Day Four.
Friday, May 27, 2005.

The cafeteria opens at 5:00 a.m. and we're expected to eat. The structure is serious here. I'm starting to get my appetite back. I still can't eat much and my hands are too shaky to use a fork, but the food is fantastic.

There's quite an assortment of characters in my program.

There's a total of eighty-four of us and approximately twenty of those people were admitted this week, like me. It feels a bit like we're playing Big Brother, all of us forming alliances. I've been mixing with everyone in this place; it is expected of us as part of the program. We aren't supposed to get too close with any one person. I've made a point to learn everyone's names. I can't believe how my short-term memory has returned. I know every single person's name in the group. When I was using, I couldn't recall details about people very easily.

I've chosen my alliance or trust circle. It consists of a female dancer, a male and female nurse, an alpha male jock, and a computer programmer. We all bring something different to the group and our backgrounds are very diverse. The one thing we all have in common is our disease and a sense of compassion. I could feel that from these people and it seemed to draw us together. I don't know anyone here. What I say or do isn't going to be in the local papers or on the news. I feel like I can let my guard down here, with the staff, and my alliance.

This morning, I checked the board outside the nurses' station to see if my privileges have been changed, and they were. I'm allowed to leave the grounds now. I need to go shopping soon.

Day Five.
Saturday, May 28, 2005.

Today was an eventful day. It was my first weekend in rehab. Most of the inhabitants were allowed to go home on therapeutic passes but that was not the case for me. My home was too far away, and to be honest I don't think they feel like I'm ready yet. I agree.

I am in desperate need of some clothes. Dancer and I decided to go shopping because it was her birthday.

We took the bus to the Stoneroad Mall. Of course, we saw the irony in the name but tried not to dwell on it. Talking about our pasts is okay but glorifying them is dangerous. It felt so strange to be out in public again. It's been less than a week since I got here, but it feels like it's been three months.

As we entered the mall, the sights and sounds were overwhelming. I felt raw and excited but also very humble. I was now walking about in a society that was providing the means for my care. I had always been the caregiver and now I was on the other side of the equation. As I looked around at our group I suddenly realized that all of us owed our lives to the segment of the populace that supports treatment for addicts. Most people don't understand or even acknowledge addiction, but, obviously, society as a whole cares.

Clothes shopping accomplished. I'm starting to like being sober.

Off to bed in my new T-shirt. (Take notes, Lorenzo. Cover it up.)

Day Six.
Sunday, May 29, 2005.

The weekends allow us a little more free time, except we must attend two twelve-step meetings and show up in the morning, early afternoon, and early evening for check-in. Addicts' lives become very unstructured and chaotic. Part of the treatment process is to introduce structure into our lives and to strongly encourage healthy activities. During the weekdays these are organized for us, but right now I have gym, billiards, tennis, horseshoes, basketball, and baseball to occupy me. There are also puzzles and chess for anyone unable to take on more physical activities.

My withdrawal symptoms are gone. So is that voice in my head that was telling me how I would use one more time when I get out. Methadone is amazing. It's a much kinder way to detox.

I tried to lift some weights with Jock yesterday, but the tendons in my mid-arm were too sore. I have huge volcano-like lesions in this area from repeated use of the same IV site. I know by looking at them that these battle scars will never completely go away.

How could I do this to my body? My parents fought so hard to keep me alive when I was sick as a child. And I've worked so hard in my adult years to be fit... Okay,

Grant. Enough beating yourself up. You can't change the past. Dancer's track marks are just as bad as yours. Not quite as deep but more distributed.

It's helping me immensely to talk about the marks with her and with others. I put on one of my new short-sleeved shirts to wear for Dancer's birthday pizza last night. It was the first time I've worn short sleeves in two years and I swear I'll never again wear long sleeves to cover my scars.

We had pizza delivered to the front door and brought it up to one of the lounge rooms. The party was fun. We all had a good laugh at the fact that we were having a pizza party in a mental institution. And then something amazing happened. Someone told a joke. I laughed. A from-the-belly-bringing-tears-to-your-eyes laugh.

I haven't laughed like that in years. It felt so...unnerving? It's been so long since I've been Grant that I really don't know who I am now. I know I'm not the Grant from my childhood, either.

When I woke up this morning, I thought of the many Sunday mornings I spent as a child, preparing for church and Sunday School. I used to be so full of this enthusiastic spirit. I was spiritual. I was never extremely religious but for most of my life I did believe. In what? I don't even know anymore. I know that recently I've been so ashamed of myself that I've had no desire to think about it. I've basically been like a child wanting to hide his sordid ways from his parents.

Silicon asked me if he could talk to me after this morning's AA meeting. His fingers are nicotine-stained and he talks with a bit of a lisp because he perforated his nasal septum due to extreme cocaine use. His demeanour this morning was so guarded that it made me a secretly excited to hear what he wanted to talk about.

His dilemma was simple, but for a newly recovering addict, it seemed shameful and hazardous. He was scared to mention it before our road trip yesterday, but he had a car parked in the lot. The look on his face said all I needed to know. This vehicle, in its present state, was not safe for him.

I immediately offered to clean it for him. This was likely reckless but I'd never even seen cocaine before, let alone used it. Besides, my selfishness saw this as a way for the group to be more mobile.

I approached the vehicle much like a SWAT team would. I felt like I was involved in a DEA take down. My heart pounded. My hands were sweating. I didn't wait to get caught with my hands on cocaine! I had enough problems to deal with.

It was a dark blue two-door Honda Accord. I thought he did well to hang onto it because it was such an old car, but after opening the door I realized it was also probably his home. The interior of the car smelled like stale cigarettes and pot.

There were dozens of coffee cups, fast-food bags, and scattered pieces of clothing.

As I started to empty things into a garbage bag, I couldn't help but notice all the CDs were out of their cases and flung all over the car. He was using the CDs' smooth surfaces to snort from.

I wiped off the CDs and put them back in their cases. I took the car to a nearby car wash and vacuumed it out, combing it like I was on an episode of CSI.

I never told him (or anyone else) about the bag of cocaine I found in the space beside the spare tire. I put it deep in the garbage bag at the car wash. He never warned me or asked me about it. I knew from my own experience that I'd hide things and never remember doing so.

He was so grateful to see his car clean that he started to cry. That made me cry. He hugged me and thanked me. Everyone hugs each other here. It was awkward at first, but I find it comforting now. Hugs not drugs.

Afterwards, I came back here and lay on my bed and closed my eyes and hugged my stiff plastic pillow. I imagined one of my daughters in my arms. The pillow-case grew damp with my tears.

One day at a time.

I wrote those words on a sheet of paper to remind myself.

Seeing the chaos that was created in my new friend's life gave me a small glimpse into my own. I can't let this overwhelm me. All that matters is that today I'm sober and I helped a recovering addict.

The buzzing in my ears has gone away. Thank goodness.

Now I lay me down to sleep.

Day Seven.
Monday, May 30, 2005.

The start of a new week means we're back into full program. We start every day with stretches in the gym that's located at the far end of the building. Stretches are followed with a brisk outdoor walk through the sprawling, picturesque grounds. It's the one time every day that all of us are in one place. We slowly walk around the gym, clockwise, doing active stretches.

I noticed a new, young pregnant girl this morning. Her breasts were basically hanging out of her shirt. The fog is lifting. I feel my natural desires emerging again. A week ago, I wouldn't have given her a second glance.

I walked today with Dancer. I don't want to spend too much time with her or they'll separate us. There's a purpose to everything they do here. They document who did the walk and who walked with whom. If you're spending too much time with any one person, they have a little chat with you. This is one of the many ways they keep tabs on us and our associations.

I had my group session this morning and at 11:30 we had our health professional group.

Bear and Danger are also in this group. (Bear is the male nurse because he reminds me of a Koala Bear.

Danger...well...she's young and cute and that's what Jock calls her.) This group meets three times a week and there is extra time in the program for anyone who's a health professional or a professional caregiver. Our group has mostly nurses, but there's a pastor, social workers, pharmacists, and physicians. It's the whole reason I was sent here. Not many institutions in Canada deal with the nuances of addicted health professionals.

The shame, professional fallout, access to meds, etc. It's a very private group and one thing that I'll say about it is that it's going to be essential to getting me well again.

The doctor who runs the group told me this morning that I'm the sickest person in here.

I almost snickered, but he looked me straight in the eye and said he was serious. Talk about breaking through a person's denial.

I had a flash of ten to twenty vivid scenes projecting on the insides of my momentarily closed eyes. That long paused blink revealed to me what he meant. I am a very sick man.

Sitting here on my bed, I reflect again on my day. Those flashes of memories I had earlier. It was like the time my short life flashed before my eyes when I was ten years old and almost drowned.

Strangely, though, the near-drowning flashes were comforting while these were horrifying.

Goodnight to me and to all of those with scary memories. May we learn to make peace with them.

Day Eight.
Tuesday, May 31, 2005.

It's the end of my second Tuesday in rehab. I spent the bulk of my day in group sessions and I played some tennis this afternoon. I can't believe I was playing tennis when I could barely walk up a set of stairs two weeks ago. The body recovers amazingly. My physical symptoms are all gone now.

I had my first Caduceus meeting today at 4 p.m. I was feeling both invigorated and nervous about it. A Caduceus meeting is where all health professionals in recovery within the greater Toronto area come together. This includes everyone who has a college overseeing their license and privileges...so pharmacists, dentists, veterinarians, registered nurses, and physicians. These people all have easy access to prescription medications and need a lot of support after recovery.

They have to attend their Caduceus meetings for at least five years after they're discharged from rehab. It's not so much a support group as an accountability group.

This is a very secretive meeting so I can't go into any details about discussions that were had, but, for example, if someone was going away on vacation, they come to Caduceus and go through every possible scenario of how they could relapse and put safeguards in place to prevent something from happening. Members of the group also have the ability to immediately call for a drug test of another member. Everyone in the group gets tested regularly anyway, but this is something else built in as a safeguard.

At first, I was intimidated. Listening to all the different titles and stories. Then I realized I wasn't the only professional to fuck up and get in trouble. I have to admit I was holding my head a little higher after leaving that room than I was when I entered it.

Health professionals are people, too, and when they develop the disease of addiction, the access they have just makes them all the more likely to become severely ill.

I think I'm getting better. This evening when I was in the hallway on my way back to bed, I wanted some ginger cookies for a snack. I snuck up the stairs to the other unit, creeping along the hallway so as not to be spotted, looking for those cookies. I could see into someone's empty room that there was a box of cookies lying on a desk. I wanted those cookies, but I couldn't do it. I couldn't take what was not mine.

Has my thinking ever changed over these nine days. I would have taken anything a couple weeks ago, especially if it would alter my mood. My moral compass must be turning around again.

Now, my body tells me it's time for sleep.

God, please take care of my children while I'm away.

Night.

Day Nine.
Wednesday, June 1, 2005.

Today was the first day I went into "recovery group."
After you're in rehab for at least a week, if the medical
team agrees that you've progressed enough that you're
ready to dig deeper, you join the recovery group. Today
was my first day there.

There are a lot of rules in recovery group:

You need to have your feet flat on the floor

No interrupting someone who's speaking

No commenting on what someone has shared

Only use your own experience when talking about something

*"What you hear and see here, let it stay here when you leave
here."*

If you ever break the rules, you're thrown out of the
group. Because of this, I will never talk about anyone's
specific story, even in my own journal. I'll only talk about
general topics we covered.

It was amazing how we all just opened up to each
other. All of us, total strangers. Every week the group
changes; people graduate and people join all the time.
Today, I shared deeper dark secrets than I've ever shared
with anyone before. These people understand me. Things
normal people would think were crazy were things these
people get. Because they would have done the same

thing in my situation. With addiction, we all do wild things. This disease wants us dead so it makes us push the boundaries of what is normal and it rips our moral fabric to shreds.

Today I met people who sold their bodies for drugs, stole for drugs, one woman even had her husband arrested, having faked domestic abuse, just so she could have him out of the house so she could keep using. I had to admit that if I was as desperate as these people without the kind of access I had, I probably would have done the same things as they did.

Addiction makes us so desperate that we're willing to do anything. I went from being a fully functional doctor who wouldn't even give his brother in withdrawal a prescription, to being an intravenous drug user. I've crossed so many lines so many times...the guilt and shame of all of it has been feeding my disease.

I'm starting to finally be able to look back, as a sober person, at what I've done, with the support of my new friends.

I see now that I was not corrupt. I was sick.

Today has been a great day. I've started the process of healing the inside of myself while the scars on my arm start to (hopefully) fade. All of this will eventually heal if I stay away from using again.

This plastic pillow I'm lying on is actually starting to feel comfortable. I feel safe again. And I thank the heavens for one more sober day.

Sweet dreams, Grant.

Day Ten.
Thursday, June 2, 2005.

So, I started smoking. I'm not proud, but 98 per cent of the people here smoke and I basically wasn't part of the group because I wasn't going out for a cigarette. So, I started. When I first got here, I would just have a cigarette once in a while, but I'm keeping up with them now. It's really the best way to stay social. I sound like a teenager making excuses for Mom and Dad, but the way I see it, it's better than shooting drugs into my vein. I'll quit when I leave this place.

On our breaks, we all go to the smoking pit and sit around talking about recovery, sometimes making fun of each other. We have our own little clique so sometimes we poke fun at the other groups huddled in the other corners in their own circles. It reminds me of inmates in prison. Our own little gangs.

We all come from a society where people have treated us like outcasts, so we are like inmates in that regard.

I don't feel like a doctor anymore. I feel more like a patient. An addict. Also, sometimes I feel like a voice of reason in my group. Maybe because my addiction didn't hit me until I was older? Maybe because I'm older and educated and haven't hit the streets yet?

I say, "not yet" because if I hadn't come here, I would have been guaranteed to be on the streets.

People look up to me because recovery seems to be coming easily to me. I feel a bit like a ringleader in our group. Like if someone were to say something about me, I would be fiercely protected. A lot of people don't like doctors in rehab because it's us who initiate medications that made them addicted. As everyone gets to know me, they realize doctors are just people. Plus, I try to explain that Big Pharma hadn't informed us well enough about the dangers of giving weeks worth of prescriptions to people.

I've been trying to reach out to other people while I'm out at the smoke pit, too. When I see someone sitting alone, I'll go and talk to them. Ask their name and find out why they're here. Not as a doctor but as a new addict in recovery. Hearing their stories makes mine make more sense. For some reason, people loosen up more in the smoking area. It's the same everywhere, I suppose. Not just rehab. I was never a smoker before, but I always saw people huddled up talking outside of buildings like they have their own little club. Now I was part of one. People share things in the smoke pit that they wouldn't within the walls of the building.

I thought about this as I was getting ready for bed, spending more time washing my hands and brushing my teeth to get rid of the stink of the cigarettes. Now as I lay down, I think about one girl I met outside today. A young girl. She said her parents disowned her because of her addiction. Because of that, she moved in with her dealer boyfriend. She became even more addicted because he kept enabling her behaviour for his own sexual satisfaction.

My heart breaks for her. I think of my own daughters and how I must get myself better so I can help make sure they don't end up down this path.

We all end up coming to the same fork in the road. The one on the left has a sign that says, "Numb away your worries." The other says, "Life on life's terms." Even though that seems a little harsher, life on life's terms is the one everyone should choose.

Drugs help us cope momentarily, but they will destroy everything in the end.

That's how I made it onto this plastic-covered mattress on a single bed.

Good night, babe.

Day Eleven. Friday, June 3, 2005.

It's Friday. Almost the end of my second week in rehab. I've been spending weekdays in groups and doing activities, but this afternoon I went for a walk with Dancer. She seemed melancholy this afternoon and wasn't walking as fast as she usually did. I asked her what was wrong and she said something came up in group that morning that reminded her of something that happened in her past.

She was driving home one night when a police officer pulled her over on the side of the road.

He knew she was an addict. He forced her into the backseat of her own car and raped her. She said he was riding her from behind with her skirt down around her knees. He was stronger than she was, and she couldn't fight him off. When he finished, he laughed and said, "You're nothing but an addict. No one's gonna believe you." He zipped himself up and went back to his car, then drove away.

She started to cry as she told me her story and I could tell she was ashamed of the fact that she put herself in that situation. I told her it wasn't her fault and what he did was extremely wrong, but more so because he was in a position of authority. Unfortunately, way too many addicts are thought of as just scum, junkies, outcasts of society. The fact of the matter is that addicts are human beings...sons, daughters, mothers, and fathers. These are people who have made a bad choice and then life spirals into a place where they (we) can no longer protect ourselves. We don't even have a voice anymore if something happens like it did to Dancer.

I encouraged her to share her story with her recovery group. Secrets keep us sick. The more we talk about these things and understand that others have gone through them, the more healing will take place.

Dancer is my best friend in here. I hate that someone did that to her.

As we kept walking, she picked up to her usual pace again. She seemed a bit lighter on her feet when she got that load off her shoulders. We both started to laugh about how people like us, from very straitlaced homes, can end up where we did. Much better to laugh than to cry about it.

We held each other's hands as we walked back to Homewood. Making sure we let go before we got too close to the grounds where we would get in trouble for doing so.

It feels good to have a connection with someone. It makes me like the place more. I'm forming more intimate connections than I had been able to when I was living a life of drugs. Your whole existence is so superficial when you're using.

Tonight, I looked at the Narcotics Anonymous book on my night table. I realized it is, indeed, a "we" program.

It's almost impossible to get through recovery without other people. No wonder I've not been successful before. Addiction tries to isolate us. When the only way to get help is by reaching out to others. Especially those who have been down this road before.

I am trying not to think about how terrified Dancer must have been when she was being raped.

My dear friend, I wish that hadn't happened to you and I'm so glad that nothing like that has ever happened to me. If she can recover from that, I can certainly recover from my past. Dancer, you've given me the strength I need to get through this. I love you to the moon and back.

Day Twelve.
Saturday, June 4, 2005.

It's Saturday, but I couldn't go home like many others, because home is very far away. I've been trying not to think about my family while I'm here because the program wants us to focus on ourselves. I'm really trying to do that. Besides, whenever I call home, I cry, so I can't do it often.

I love Scarlett and my three sweet girls so much. My youngest is only two years old and she doesn't understand what's going on.

I've put my family through so much over the past couple of years... I knew what they said to me here must be true. That to put up with someone like me, Scarlett must be a very sick woman.

I spent much of the day wandering around the grounds by myself, and when I got hungry around lunchtime I went for a walk to find something to eat. I found a pizza joint and ordered a twelve-inch veggie pizza. The kind Scarlett and I usually share. I took it back with me to the beautiful grounds of Homewood and found a picnic table at the lowest level of the property.

I looked above me at the three tiers of grass and bush- es and the beautiful flowers in front of the sprawling old structure. I set down the two plastic glasses, and the one-litre bottle of Diet Coke I'd ordered, next to the pizza. I poured a glass for me and one for Scarlett, as if she were there with me. I feel responsible for the progression of her addiction.

They say I'm sick but I've been feeling so ashamed for all the things I've done. All the grief I've caused those around me. My family, friends, colleagues, and my patients. I've done them wrong. And I am sorry.

I looked across the table as if Scarlett was sitting there, and I said, "I'm sorry for all of this." I cried.

Others were going home to see their families, and not only was I too far away to see mine, but I am still too ashamed to face them.

I toasted Scarlett's glass with mine. This time, no wine. Only pop. I recalled, one time, her spilling wine on a table at a restaurant. I was so mad and aghast at the waste of wine that I almost licked it off the table. My God, what had I become? I was always such a good date. Polite, gentlemanly, able to carry a conversation. Always ready to pay the bill.

I wanted to be him again. That Grant. I knew I could be him again. Substances have robbed me of that just like so many other things. I'm determined now to get it back and to be that man again.

I never did eat any of that pizza. I couldn't bring myself to have a single bite. But our little fake date made me think deeply about the people at home who were counting on me, and how I must work on my recovery while I'm here.

I want to be that person again. The person someone would be proud to go to dinner with. I'm starting to feel like that might be possible.

Good night, Scarlett. I love you!

Day Thirteen.
Sunday, June 5, 2005.

This morning I had my regular morning check-in and then went to one of my two compulsory twelve-step meetings that we have on weekends. Bear, Dancer, and I decided afterwards to wander off to check out the town of Guelph.

As we meandered through the streets, we noticed a man sitting alone in the square outside the mall. He asked us if we were buying. We realized he'd noticed our purple hospital bracelets. I thought to myself, "That's pretty sick." This guy knows we're in rehab and that's why he's targeting us. We all know that just a few weeks ago, we would have taken him up on it.

Bear wanted to go into the mall to buy something for his wife, so Dancer and I decided to go get something to eat.

One of the rules of rehab is to not dine at licensed establishments, but the only place we could find that fit that description was a Pita Pit. Dancer didn't feel like pitas, so she talked me into going into a pub. We found a booth way in the back corner. We sat across from each other. I was feeling mischievous about what we were doing, but, at the same time, being in that atmosphere made me feel uneasy. I tried to focus on our conversation to keep my mind off it.

She told me about her days as a dancer and how she had lost so much because of her addiction. Her latest boyfriend had been a drug dealer. Another reason why the cop thought he could rape her without consequence. I started to look at her in a whole new way today. She's my friend but I'm developing feelings for her.

I've never had feelings for anyone since I met Scarlett.

These aren't feelings like I had with Scarlett, but they're feelings nonetheless. Until now I've been existing in this altered state of reality where I've had no ability to feel deeply about anything, really.

My feelings during my addiction were superficial. Not even true feelings. More like reactions to enable my sick behaviour to continue.

As I looked at Dancer today, I felt an overwhelmingly warm feeling of compassion. She's tall and attractive. I haven't noticed that before.

It was amazing that two people with such bad needle-marked arms could be having such a great time laughing over French fries. Others in the pub were looking at us like they thought we were cute together. If only they could have seen the two of us a couple weeks ago!

I can't help but think of Scarlett. Will I feel the same way for her when I return home? Our lives have become so very codependent. If I'm having feelings like this for Dancer, what does that say about my relationship? A relationship that has been built completely upon a shared addiction.

The Homewood people were right when they told us we might try to substitute other things for our substance of choice. Is Dancer my substitution?

I'm ready to turn off my light now. The bright glow from the bulb will still be in front of me when I close my eyes and rest my head on my pillow. It's amazing that when the rods and cones of the retina are stimulated by light that the brightness continues for seconds after you close your eyes.

Relationships are supposed to be the same way. That image of the person and the feelings you have for them are supposed to continue until you see them again. It's what keeps our feelings in check when we are apart. Sobriety is giving me clear enough thinking to re-evaluate why that bright spot seems so dim. Today's meal was the second date of my Homewood experience and it has left me wondering exactly what I am feeling. You know Dasher and Dancer. Sleep tight.

Day Fourteen.
Monday, June 6, 2005.

This is the start of my third week at Homewood. Last week they moved me downstairs because I guess I can be trusted a bit more now. My new roommate is another Italian guy. He's hilarious and loves sports. Especially the Cleveland Browns. I call him Cleveland.

There's another guy on our floor, with astonishingly blue eyes and blond hair. He's a rascal. He likes to glorify the old days of using and I know he shouldn't be doing that. That is a dangerous line to walk. It's one thing to talk about your past experiences, but exalting them is very triggering for yourself and for those around you.

Yesterday, Blue Eyes and three others went to one of the gorges for a swim. He took one of the young nurses. Not the one I typically hang around with. He tried to take another girl, too, but she realized what was going on and she got out of the van very quickly. They were planning to use.

Obviously, using while in program is not tolerated, so he and the other guy who picked up the drugs were asked to leave Homewood. I felt bad at first but then realized he was putting us all in jeopardy. I identified with him because he also had three daughters and was only in his late thirties.

I'm journaling about this today because I just found out he overdosed and died last night.

Those blue eyes will never shine again. His kids are left without a father.

We're all devastated. Cleveland and I talked tonight about how lucky we are that it wasn't us. So many addicts relapse and go back to the same dose they used before. Their tolerance has dropped in the meantime, causing them to inadvertently overdose.

We talked about how this place is like a reality show— except, for us, the consequences are all too real.

I plan to get up early tomorrow and go to the gym to shoot some hoops before morning walk. I'm very sad about Blue Eyes but we almost get hardened to an addict dying because it's so common. I am going to not allow his death to be in vain. It has just made me more adamant to stay on track.

Nighty night, Blue Eyes.

Day Fifteen.
Tuesday, June 7, 2005.

Today it was my turn to speak at recovery group. I've been thinking about what's really been bothering me. I keep coming back to my brother's death.

I've dealt with it very poorly, drowning myself with drugs and trying to numb away the guilt and pain. Now that I'm sober, all of my feelings about it are so over-whelming.

I explained the situation to my group today. What had happened and how I was almost angry with him for putting me in that situation in the first place. I felt guilty then about being angry with him.

Others in the group shared their similar stories. It made me feel less alone, knowing that others have experienced loss, causing them to either relapse or to have their addiction accelerate.

The facilitator of the group asked me to write a letter to bring to the meeting tomorrow. I just finished writing it tonight, on a yellow legal pad.

"Guy. You were four-and-a-half years older than me. Much bigger than me. You always protected me. I always looked up to you my entire life. I felt so helpless when I saw you not doing well, and instead of helping you, I pulled away from you. It wasn't because I didn't care about you, it's just that I've always seen you as my hero and I didn't know how to help you. That day, when I turned you away? I wish I'd been more empathetic, but I don't blame myself anymore, Guy. I really believe that when you woke up that morning, you were destined to die that day. I don't know why I believe that, but I do. If nothing else, it helps me get some peace.

"It's funny. The week before you died, you told me that you loved me, probably for the first time in ten years. It was almost like you knew something was going to happen. Maybe you did."

"I love you and hope to see you someday in heaven. Your only brother, Grant."

Day Sixteen.
Wednesday, June 8, 2005.

I'm discovering that many of the people in here also have other issues. Not only are they addicted to drugs, but there are other conditions such as post traumatic stress disorder (PTSD), depression, anxiety, anorexia, or other mood disorders. A psychiatrist sees these patients regularly to help them with these issues. There's a special unit here for eating disorders, and PTSD that people go to (if needed) after their time in the addictions (HADS) unit.

One of the issues I've observed is that many of us have resentments. I guess it's one of the reasons that resentments are in the twelve steps.

My recovery group facilitator asked us to bring a little rock and closed-toed shoes to our session today. I couldn't figure out why, but I obliged.

We were told to place the rock in our shoe and walk around for the day. She asked us later that day to share what we'd discovered. The only thing that I'd noticed was that, at first, the rock wasn't uncomfortable. It was just annoying. Then, it became increasingly sore, to the point where it was just hurting me. All I had to do was take it and throw it away and it would be okay.

She explained that this is how resentment works. We choose to hold on to resentments when we can just let them go at any time, and the pain goes with them. When we let go, they can't hurt us anymore.

That's why we wrote those letters yesterday. Whether it's a letter, or a conversation about how we're being treated, letting go of resentment is powerful.

Today, we learned to talk to that person for whom we're holding resentment, about how they're making us feel. Not about confronting them about how they wronged us, but how they made us feel. Because, you can't argue with someone about how they make you feel.

When you're talking about your own feelings, you're certainly entitled to let someone know they made you feel that way. This has been a big step for me. I've never thought about this before. I'm now acutely aware that I may have hurt people.

The other part of this is that I've allowed so many people to cross my boundaries because of my people-pleasing tendencies. I've never let them know how they were making me feel (overwhelmed).

Tonight, I'm going to bed feeling less overwhelmed. I'm not going to allow people to affect my mental health by putting too much on me. I will no longer allow the trickle effect that has on my family. I have to learn how to use a word that is hard for me to say: "No."

It's 11:30 p.m. now. Lights out. Please help me to learn to say no when it's in my best interest.

Grant me the ability to say no gracefully.

Day Seventeen.
Thursday, June 9, 2005.

I'm now smoking half a pack a day. I'm going to have some work to do when I get out. But I've detoxed from opioids, so nicotine should be a breeze, right? I'll worry about that in eleven days from now.

There are twelve-step meetings every day at Homewood. They're either in the physical Homewood building, or somewhere within walking distance. They consist of Narcotics Anonymous, Alcoholics Anonymous, Cocaine Anonymous, and Gamblers Anonymous. I've attended all the different meetings, just to get a feel for what they're like. I also want to feel comfortable in the rooms of all the meetings just in case I ever need them in the future. The Narcotics Anonymous is the meeting I've attended most. It takes place in the basement of Homewood and is chaired by this tall Latino guy who's missing one ear.

I'm so curious about what happened to his ear. A lot of people here have had drug debt and have been beaten up or maimed in an attempt to collect or to send a message. Some people still owe money and that's where their sponsor comes in. The sponsor will often accompany someone back to pay the debt. It's very dangerous to go back into a drug house alone in early sobriety. Dealers will often offer free samples to get recovering addicts back as customers. Or so I'm told.

A lot of people who live around Guelph pick up sponsors while in Homewood. I made a phone call home to find mine. The thought of going to meetings back home makes me cringe. It's such a small place and everyone knows me as Dr. Matheson. But I'll cross that bridge when I come to it. Now I'm just happy to have someone. He's been sober for twenty-four years.

The profile of the people coming into Homewood is changing. There are a lot of cross-addicted individuals. There are two types of meetings. One was the speaker meeting in which a person stands up and shares his or her story with the crowd. The other is discussion style where we break into groups, sit in circles, and take turns talking about our day and what's on our mind. Some people don't like meetings, but I do.

I try to focus on our similarities and not our differences.

One man at a speaker meeting told us a story about how twenty years ago he backed over his nephew with his car, killing him. Even twenty years later, he still cries.

I immediately thought, that could have happened to me.

I know these meetings are going to be an important part of my recovery. For the first year I will go often because it will help me, and I'll be able to lend an ear to someone else in time of need.

These twelve-step programs are often said to be spiritual-based and they are. But spiritual is completely different than religious. Your higher power can be what-ever you want it to be. For me, it's about the energy of all living things in the universe. That's my higher power.

I'm asking this higher power to just help me to do the right thing, and not to use.

I need to reprogram my thinking and use this energy to somehow help me do that one day at a time.

God grant me the serenity.

Day Eighteen.
Friday, June 10, 2005.

Today was a beautiful day. Homewood staff put on a barbecue for patients, as they do every second Friday.

There's a small building on the lower field, next to the baseball diamond. Kitchen staff brought all the burgers, sausages, hotdogs, toppings, and salads there. The building is nestled in the trees, juxtaposed to the tennis courts and the horseshoe pits. It looked like it was built in the 1800s. I saw a picture of it from the early 1900s on the Homewood wall and I think it might have been a lodge of some type.

The side of the building facing the ball field has a covered porch with four long white benches. I was sitting there watching the festivities when Dancer came and sat beside me. She said, "What are you going to have to eat?" I told her I wasn't sure. She said, "Well, you could always have me! Ha ha!"

I laughed. We were flirtatious with each other, but nothing was going to come from it. We grabbed some burgers and joined our friends to listen to their ongoing troubles.

I decided to open up about something that's been bothering me. I told my friends that I was worried about being released because my girlfriend is still using my drug of choice. I did urge her to try and stop while I was here, but she can't. And she doesn't seem to want to.

I didn't tell any of the staff about this because they probably wouldn't release me back to my home, and I have three children to consider.

Everyone agreed that I was facing an impossible situation. My friends told me that the best I can do is to be an example for Scarlett, and let her see that I'm leading a better life. Hopefully she will reach out and ask me for help.

It felt good to talk about my concerns.

I know Scarlett is sick and doesn't mean to put me in a bad situation. But I'm responsible for my own recovery. I have to do what I can to keep myself safe because if not? We'll both likely end up dead.

So many addicts inject themselves, nod off, and never wake up.

Please God don't let that happen to my Scarlett.

Day Nineteen.
Saturday, June 11, 2005.

A fellow patient (a nurse from BC) came to me today with a proposition. She wanted to travel to Niagara Falls but she didn't want to go by herself. Someone on staff suggested my name to her because I can't go home on the weekends anyway. I didn't want to go with a female alone, so I agreed on the condition that I could invite some other people.

There's one person here I really want to get to know better. Lonzo. He was admitted a week before me and he is one scary-looking motherfucker. He's about 6'5" and probably 280 pounds and he just looks angry all the time. He's the kind of guy you would not want to cross in an alley. You might even cross the street to avoid walking past him.

I can tell he's been in a lot of rough situations and I've been wanting to know more of his story.

He agreed to join us if he could bring a friend. An English guy.

We must have been quite the sight getting in the car today. This middle-aged nurse, me weighing about 155 pounds soaking wet, Lonzo the monster, and the chatty Englishman.

Off we went to Niagara Falls. We all wanted to get a good close look at the falls, so we got on one of the boats, put on our raincoats, and went out almost right underneath the waterfall. What an experience. Seeing the massive amounts of water pouring over the falls made me feel so small and insignificant. I thought about how this feat of nature has been occurring for thousands and thousands of years. I'm just a speck in all of this. But, I'm responsible for this little speck. I realized this is my chance to turn things around. Just like someone who's been travelling around lost, I have the opportunity now to decide to change my course.

Sometimes I feel like it's easier to plow ahead even if things are getting worse and worse. I think that's my ego. Seeing that massive display of water pouring over those rocks made me realize how small yet important I am. My ego needs to be deflated and I have to admit that I need to change.

It probably seemed insignificant to most people, how I accepted the raincoat to go out on that boat today, but taking that cautionary step reminded me of how sensible I am now compared to a few weeks ago. One night while I was drunk, I climbed outside the window of our room in a high-rise hotel and proceeded to walk on a one-foot ledge all around the hotel. I don't know how I didn't fall. If I had, I would have plunged to my death.

I remember discovering the bruises on the insides of my thighs from climbing over the glass railings, and realizing I'd done something dangerous and foolish.

Our group became close today. Especially Lonzo and I. We're so different, but those differences slip away when you talk about your addiction with someone. We've come from completely different backgrounds but we're here in this same place.

I think about that now as I tuck myself into bed.

I wonder if I'd never picked up a substance what my life would be like. Might be better. Might be worse. Something more tragic might have happened to me if I didn't become an addict. Maybe I would be in a plane crash. Maybe I would have a sick or injured child.

I can't dwell on things like this. I have to try and enjoy this day. I guess that's why they tell us to live one day at a time and to not dwell on the past or fear the future.

I enjoyed the splendor of Niagara Falls today with my recovery friends, sober and at peace.

Day Twenty.
Sunday, June 12, 2005.

I think I've written before about how we have to attend two meetings on the weekends. What I didn't mention was how, on Sunday mornings, you can choose church instead of a meeting.

I haven't been to church in years. I've been too ashamed to even walk in front of a church.

I'm a grown-up. A minister's son who played in churches as a child and listened to countless sermons over my lifetime. When I was using, I felt like a leper and wouldn't go inside a church. I know it sounds strange, but that's what I believed.

I decided today would be different.

I made my way down through the grounds of Homewood, walking past the beautiful greenery and flowers. It's so pretty here.

I exited through the back gate which I suspect at one time was closed. It looked like there was a guard station there in the past.

I meandered through the streets of Guelph and headed up across the footbridge into the town. We weren't allowed to have our phones so I couldn't Google anything, so I looked up a Presbyterian Church at Homewood and got the address before I left. All I wanted was to sit in the building and not be noticed, but I enjoyed the service. I found myself singing the hymns and really paying attention to the message.

Singing always makes me feel happier. It's like a release of energy. And it made me feel at peace today. I didn't feel tormented or paranoid. I felt happy.

On my way back I met up with some of my friends who were sitting around the smoke pit. Silicon, Dancer, Bear, Young Nurse (a new character in our crew), and I all went for a walk. Young Nurse is fresh out of school and got herself into some trouble I won't get into. She has a good heart, but being young and beautiful and addicted, she made a great target for some bad people.

We went to the convenience store to get some slushies. I got another bag of Smartfood popcorn. I've eaten one every day since I got here. I don't know why. It hasn't put any weight on me. I guess it's all the walking.

I am starting to ramble. I guess today was a bonding day and we have those in recovery sometimes. My emotions are all over the place right now, and I'm getting better at talking about them with my friends instead of burying them, which has only led to trouble for me in the past.

I feel at peace now.

Goodnight, Alex Grant.

Day Twenty-One.
Monday, June 13, 2005.

Today was Monday, which meant group team rounds. It's like a regular meeting, but we have a full health team here with us. There are six health professionals per group of fourteen patients and the health team consists of a physician, nurse, nutritionist, recreational therapist, addiction therapist, and social worker.

The physicians tend to lead the groups, and the team physician in my group is a very robust man with a way about him that just exudes confidence. I respect him immensely.

At the beginning of the meeting today, the doctor went around the room asking if anyone wanted time to talk to the group. I said I would like to say something. When the time came for me to talk, I had a crying fit as I was trying to explain what was bothering me so much.

It was Scarlett. I was still afraid to divulge to the staff about her active addiction, but I did. I just poured out my heart, about how I am afraid to go back home.

I love her so much, but with an active addiction in the house I was second-guessing my feelings. I know I love her, but with me sober, I don't know if what we had will ever be the same. I was sharing this with the group and I was so upset.

The doctor looked at me from across the room and threw me a set of keys. I caught them. He asked me to look through the keys and pick the one I thought was the most appealing.

I went through the keys, looking at them carefully. I picked a thick, bright little key because it had some ornamental details on it. I told him that's the one I choose.

He said, great. Go over to the door and insert the key in the lock.

So, I took the key and crossed the room. I tried a few times to put the key in the lock, but it didn't fit.

I didn't get the point at first, but many in the group got it right away.

I walked over and stood in front of him and shrugged. Telling him I didn't understand.

He said, "Grant, sometimes the things we think are best for us, don't turn out to be the right fit."

I have to go back home reassessing my relationship. It's going to be very difficult to live with a drug addict and remain sober.

Tonight, I say a prayer for my family. We make a lot of choices in life and who knows what exactly is the right fit? I know one thing for certain. The right fit does not involve ending up in rehab for an IV narcotic addiction.

Bedtime now.

Goodnight, John Boy.

Day Twenty-Two.
Tuesday, June 14, 2005.

Lonzo left today. When someone graduates from here, or completes the program, they get a pin. They can ask someone in their group to pin them and say a few words. I was honoured when Lonzo asked me.

We stood in the middle of the group, twelve people around us, and I tried to express to him what he has meant to me and how his example has helped me through my journey.

I started to cry. I could barely get the words out of my mouth. We hugged each other and when he stepped back, he said he chose me because I'm the person here who surprised him the most. That he thought this doctor would think he's so much better than everyone else. But he learned what I already knew. That I'm no different than anyone else.

I was again honoured that he felt this way. I feel like I'm just one more survivor on this lifeboat, trying to make it after the ship sank.

On the lifeboat, it doesn't matter what you are or who you are. You're just trying to survive and that's what I feel like here. Lonzo is a sharp guy and he spotted this in me. It makes me feel good that he did.

I feel proud tonight going to bed.

Proud that I got to pin my friend. Proud I haven't gotten myself in any relationships. And proud I haven't used today.

Goodnight, Full Moon.

Day Twenty-Three.
Wednesday, June 15, 2005.

This afternoon was recreation time. It was beautiful outside so we went down to the ball field. There's a volleyball net, tennis courts, horseshoe pits, baseball, soccer, and basketball equipment. A group of us decided to play volleyball. I am amazed at the physical recovery I've made since I got here. In a little more than three weeks, I've gone from barely being able to walk up a set of stairs to being able to run up a steep set of stairs two or three steps at a time.

The track marks are starting to heal, though I suspect I'll have lifelong scars. Dancer's are just as bad, if not worse. I think that's one of the reasons I was drawn to her. She makes me feel better about myself. Or at least like we're on equal footing.

Intravenous drug users tend to talk to each other here because there's a whole other side of the addiction. The needles (which we call rigs), the tourniquet, the cooking... it's all a ritual that becomes an addiction in itself.

Anyway, back to volleyball. I'm amazed at how these people I saw shuffling into Homewood are now playing a vigorous game of volleyball. The competitiveness is pretty incredible. We all worked up a pretty good sweat, both because of the exercise and because it's hot outside.

It was my turn to go off as a substitute, and I took the time to just sit back and watch them. A month ago, these people were living life in disarray. Back then, they were physically, mentally, and spiritually bankrupt. Somehow, we all ended up in this wonderful place, able to enjoy each other's company and work together to get a ball over a net. It doesn't seem like much, but three weeks ago that would have been impossible for me. Not only physically, but I wouldn't have been able to work with others like this.

I'm glad these rooms are air-conditioned. My bedroom would be very warm if it wasn't. It makes it easier to sleep. I'm able to sleep better now. I can focus more on being in the moment.

I listen to the hum of the air conditioner now instead of the noise in my head that always made me feel uncomfortable. That bad feeling is quiet now.

Keep me safe until morning light.

Day Twenty-Four.
Thursday, June 16, 2005.

Today in recovery group, we were asked to bring the letters we'd written. I had mine to my brother. Others had some to people who had harmed them, or against whom they have resentments. We all took these letters outside to the fire pit. One at a time, we slowly approached the fire and put our letters on the flame and watched them go up in smoke.

There was so much grief, anger, and pain. But somehow, sharing this together and watching the fire consume our words helped us to heal.

Drug use made me focus on all of the negatives in my life and it just made them all worse.

I remember the pain I suffered when I was in withdrawal. Now here I am without an ache or pain in my body. Including the heartache.

I've been blaming myself for my brother's death for so many years. Every time I've seen Mom cry about it, I've wanted to crawl into a hole. It's hard to pretend you're this important doctor when you feel so low and unworthy. But I wasn't feeling like that anymore. This place has been healing me and for the first time in a very long time, I have hope.

We all joined hands around the fire and said the serenity prayer. The leader of the group said this is just the beginning of our journey and we should all journal anytime we're feeling uncomfortable or even happy. Seeing things on paper sometimes helps us with our feelings. I know that since I've been journaling, I often don't know I'm feeling something until it spills out on the page.

It's hard to put into words how much recovery group has helped me. I feel safe there. Like I can talk about anything. And the more I talk, the more others share their own secrets. There's been a lot of healing in that group. I know that when I go home, I'm going to be under a lot of public scrutiny. I need to be strong to face that. I guess not so much strong as able and willing to let things go, and try not to worry about what people think of me.

I love the expression, "What others think of me is none of my business."

Goodnight, Me.

Day Twenty-Five.
Friday, June 17, 2005.

Today was the beginning of my last weekend here and it was beautiful. The weather was sunny and about 26°C.

I attended the Native AA meeting this morning. It's unique in that we sit in a circle and anyone entering the room must go around the circle and not cross through it. The person who is speaking must have the speaking stick which is passed to whoever wants to share.

They refer to the higher power as the great spirit. I noticed that Dancer wasn't at the meeting. I had been looking for her earlier to see if she would walk down with me. The meeting was off grounds about half a kilometre along the river. The route takes you along a zigzagging path and a long cement wall that is covered with graffiti. I've always liked graffiti for some reason.

I like to walk down this path with Dancer. She always has unique perspectives on the artwork. It felt strange that she wasn't here today and, somehow, I could sense there was something wrong.

Earlier in the week she told me she loves to walk into a room where I am already present.

I asked her why. She explained, "Because I can feel your eyes on me from the minute I enter the room until the second I leave."

I told her I didn't even realize that and she laughed. She also told me that day that she felt better than she has since she was twelve years old. I was so happy for her.

Almost overnight her attitude seemed to change. She had been different through the later part of the week. I thought a lot of it was the anticipation of going home. She was going back to live in a bad situation. She could share a lot of her stories with her recovery group and also with me. I felt privileged to be her friend. She is so animated, so emotional, yet blunt. I have really felt her dodging me this week. She's been hanging around with different crowd. People who were just admitted and were still very sick.

As I came back from the meeting, I saw Dancer. She was walking through the parking lot towards a vehicle that was parked just outside the grounds. I met up with her. She told me her boyfriend had dropped off the car this morning. He wasn't even going to drive her home. She had to drive herself.

She told me she was leaving today, despite her discharge date being Tuesday. I tried to talk her into staying but I could tell she was determined to leave. I gave her a hug and she whispered in my ear, "I had to pull away from you."

I asked her what she meant but she wouldn't answer. She said, "I can give you a drive to the airport when you leave, if you want me to." I told her I would like that very much. One more hug and she was gone.

I know what her leaving today means and it makes me

extremely sad. I can see signs of relapse with the justification of leaving early, and the timing of it being on the weekend, quite possibly to hang out with some of the recently admitted people who would be out on pass.

I thought about her a lot today and into the evening. I talked to Bear about her. He always had a good sense of reason and said, "You know Dancer." It was very simple but true. We have to detach with love when people are in those situations.

We ourselves can get very sick by trying to be caretakers, especially when we are early in recovery.

Dancer had achieved so much growth in the time she was here. I care about her so much, and I'm very sad to think that she may be going back out into that same life again.

This place seems a little emptier without, her but I have to focus on my own recovery. My heart broke a little today. But I could feel it, and I was able to talk about it with a friend.

I will never forget the impact she had on my recovery, and I will be forever grateful to her for getting me through some of my toughest days here.

Perhaps in some roundabout way she wasn't here for herself but she was here to help me in my journey.

Goodnight, Dancer. Keep safe.

Day Twenty-Six.
Saturday, June 18, 2005.

Today I was concentrating on observing my friends. Enjoying their progress helps me to appreciate my own. Silicon was talking less about the guilt he felt towards his family and how he lost them by snorting cocaine. We'd taken his car several times for our little outings. It was nice having a vehicle at our disposal.

I see everyone growing and progressing now. It's amazing how I have grown to love these people. I've never been in a place where so many people have suffered such trauma, most of it by their own hand, but some at the hands of others.

I guess, to make a normal person understand how desperate an addict becomes, would be to ask you, "What would you do if you were starving?"

That's how an addict feels. As if they were going to die if they don't do something about the situation right away.

It's amazing to watch these people that I've grown to care for, progress from a state of reckless and impulsive thinking to a state where they consider others before themselves.

I've heard a term here many times: "Progress, not perfection."

For me, it meant that if I'm trying to work my program to the best of my ability and then I falter, it's okay. As well, we must be easy on each other but we have to point out when we see the disease taking back control. I witnessed that firsthand today from a young girl I didn't know very well. She found out she couldn't see her kids this weekend and she went into quite a state. Everything was negative. She wouldn't talk to anyone. She isolated herself and started blaming everyone else for her situation. I know the staff tried to talk to her but she got on the phone with her friends and then basically walked out.

There's nothing keeping us here. We're all here because we put ourselves here.

People who leave rehab don't do well. Anytime you put something before your recovery? You lose it in the end.

Another 24 down.

Day Twenty-Seven.
Sunday, June 19, 2005.

It's hard not being able to go home on the weekends. It's now the third Sunday in June. Father's Day. Some kids came today to see their dads. Mine live too far away.

My time here is coming to an end, but today I felt glum. A few of us were down playing pool in the recreation area. They have these enormous antique pool tables here that date back to the 1800s. We were in the middle of a game when a father and his son of about fourteen years old came into the gym area. His son wanted to get on the treadmill but it was turned up way too fast. His father warned him he was increasing the speed, but the boy didn't listen. Before any of us could react, the boy fell and was thrown from the treadmill against the wall. The treadmill track rubbed against his face as he was pinned between it and the wall. He had quite an abrasion on his cheek. His father picked up him up and carried him out. Oh my god. It was all we could do, to contain our laughter.

How many times have we all been in that situation, ignoring words of warning just to do the exact same thing that kid did, falling flat on our faces. The irony was apparent to all of us.

I got a call from the nurses' station today that a package arrived for me. It was searched, as per standard protocol, but all it contained were some pictures and letters. Pictures of Scarlett and my three daughters. My parents and my sister. I read through the letters in my room. The one that touched me most was the one from my twelve-year-old. At the end, she wrote, "I can sleep at night now, knowing that you are safe."

Until then I didn't realize how my illness had been affecting my family, especially my children. I had always been the golden boy. The perfect father, the perfect doctor. Now I had to build up that trust all over again.

I look around me at the walls of this room and I feel overwhelmed, but I am alive and healthy. I am not responsible for my addiction, but I am responsible for my recovery. Maybe someday my story will help someone else. May prevent them from going down this path, or to find help if they do.

In AA, they say, "You can get off the garbage truck anytime. You don't have to take it all the way to the dump." What that means is that you don't have to lose everything before you can seek help. AA meetings and NA meetings are everywhere. If someone came to me for help, I would tell them to find a meeting, even if you *think* you might have a problem. They're always welcoming.

I think back to that kid on the treadmill. It was hilarious, mostly because he wasn't badly hurt. One minute I'm laughing at someone else's misfortune and the next I'm crying at my own. I'm going to focus on the things I still have and not on what I have lost. I still have my children and family. A woman who loves me. A driver's license. A license to practice medicine. That's conditional on me coming here, so I assume it's still in place. It doesn't matter anyway because I'm not going back to work anytime soon. I have a lot to be grateful for. And gratitude is the key to happiness. Try wanting just what you have and not what you don't.

Good night, Daddy.

Day Twenty-Eight.
Monday, June 20, 2005.

It's the day before I am set to complete rehab. It was a day of reflection for me. I spent most of it walking around the grounds. I thought about the different conversations I had in all the different locations here, with so many different people.

I had heard their stories and identified so much with their situations.

I had talked to the newcomers as they came in and said the same things that were said to me when I first arrived. That it gets better, that we have to live one day at a time. To take advantage of the nursing staff and talk to them when you need to. To talk in groups and ask for time to speak whenever you can. This is a place to heal. I felt everyone I met here had a part in my healing.

The horticultural projects I completed made me feel so satisfied. And the ceramic dog I made for Beth. They were important steps in my recovery.

I'm starting to feel afraid. I'm scared to go back to the real world. I've been safe here, protected from my temptations.

I think about Scarlett and how I will make it if she's still using. I used to have to inject her myself sometimes. I won't be able to do that anymore.

She says she's quitting. That she'll clean up when I get home. I want to believe her.

Couples that use together become very codependent. Using becomes so much a part of their lives that when the drugs are gone, the relationship usually ends.

I hope and pray this isn't the case for us.

I think again about how much we all impact each other here. After being through this experience, I realize if I ever get into trouble again, I will come back to a place like this. A place that specializes in the help I need as a medical professional.

One more night on this plastic-covered mattress and pillow.

I think of Dancer again and hope she's okay. I think of Scarlett and hope the same thing.

Good night, Girls.

Day Twenty-Nine.
Tuesday, June 21, 2005.

Today was supposed to be my last day at Homewood. (I asked to stay an extra day because tomorrow evening they're having the annual Homewood reunion. Anyone who has attended Homewood can come back anytime, to this huge auditorium, and be there for the ceremony. I thought it would be good for me to see all these successful graduates of Homewood all in one place before I must go back into the real world.)

Our closing ceremony was held in front of the rest of the Homewood patients. There were fifteen of us leaving Homewood and receiving buttons or pins. Dancer was supposed to be among the group, but won't be because of her early departure.

The group selected me as the person to give the address for the group.

As we all lined up on stage I looked at all the faces in the crowd. I've been trying for four weeks and could never locate the young guy with the garbage bag I met on admission day. I'm not sure if his funding didn't come through or he just decided to leave, but I never laid eyes on him again.

It was like I imagined the whole interaction.

Everyone gave a quick talk and goodbyes and thank yous were spoken, especially to the staff and the doctors. Then it was my turn to address the group.

I hadn't prepared anything to say, so I just closed my eyes for a second and then began to speak. I talked about the relationships that I had forged since I arrived here. The strange faces in the crowd became actual people. Drugs had robbed me of the ability to think of anything else except the task at hand and my drug of choice. I thus isolated myself and became paranoid.

My relationships then became very superficial. Here I learned that by opening up and really listening to others I could heal the part of me that needed to be cared for despite my flaws. I didn't have to pretend I was the Golden Boy anymore. I was just Grant trying to do the best I could each day. And really for all of us in recovery that is all we should ask of ourselves. Take time to talk to one another and love each other well again.

Day Thirty.
Wednesday, June 22, 2005.

Most of the people from my admission week left yesterday, but Silicon and I both wanted to attend the annual meeting that happened to be scheduled for tonight. I spent most of the day visiting the people who've helped me on this journey. I spoke with my addiction counsellor, my doctor, the nurses, and other staff members. They basically saved my life and I'm very grateful. I wanted to make sure they knew that.

Anyone who's ever been a patient at Homewood is welcome to attend the AGM. There were at least four hundred people in the room. Like with most meetings there was a speaker there with fifteen years of sobriety. He talked about coming to Homewood broken, and what life has been like since then.

One of the last items on the agenda was what they called a countdown. They asked the person with the most sobriety to stand up. It was a man with 40 years under his belt. They worked their way down through the years. "Anyone with 39 years, 38 years, etc. I stood up when they said 29 days. I felt such pride! I was sober almost 30 days! The countdown went on. They got to 24 hours. Then the people who were admitted yesterday and today stood up at that time.

I couldn't help but think that that was me just a month ago. It's good to see the program worked for so many people.

I finally feel free again. I was hoping the meeting would give me the strength I need to face realities of life back on PEI. As a patient of Homewood, I could truly focus on myself, but now I have to face life as an addicted physician in recovery.

I knew since I got here that things would never be the same, but I can't let that occupy my mind. I just had to face life on life's terms, and not linger in the past or the future, but to stay in the present.

Silicon and I took a drive around Guelph one last time. We were listening to music and both singing at the top of our lungs. I imagine surviving a narcotic addiction is like returning home from war. Not that I would dare compare myself to a brave veteran, but I do feel like we have pulled through a battle. Not an armored battle but another type of war. A war that took most of our most precious things from us and almost cost us our lives.

Silicon and I talked for hours in the car. He thanked me again for cleaning out his car when we first got here. I told him it helped me to help him and that's the way most things are in recovery. He offered me a drive the following day to the airport and I told him I might have to take him up on that offer. Dancer was supposed to pick me up but I hadn't heard from her since she left so I wasn't counting on her.

Deep down inside, I hoped she would. If nothing else

it would let me know that she was doing well. I packed my clothes before I went to bed. I looked again at that long-sleeved light-blue shirt that I first wore when I got here. I was baffled by the number of the speckles of bloodstains it had. How was I unable to see them before? I'd been walking around in such a fog.

I can hear my roommate breathing in his sleep. Tomorrow night I'll be home in my own bed. I'll have to find a whole new group of recovery friends. I hope I am as successful at forming alliances with people in recovery at home as I have been here.

I have this uncomfortable feeling in my stomach tonight. Something I haven't felt in a long while. I think it's fear. Fear of the unknown.

May Angels watch me through the night.

Day Thirty-one.
Thursday, June 23, 2005.

This will be my last rehab journal entry.

I'm writing this from the window seat of an airplane. I didn't want to be in the aisle because I can't handle the drink cart. I pulled out my journal to keep my mind busy. The guy beside me ordered a double scotch and it's taking all my strength not to reach over and drink it. And I know I wouldn't be able to stop at one drink.

Dancer was supposed to pick me up at 1:30 today but she didn't show up. I had to ask Silicon for a ride to the airport. I hate to jump to conclusions, but I'm pretty sure Dancer's back at it again. A part of me is very sad because she told me a week ago that she feels better than she has since she was twelve years old.

My seatmate is in the bathroom and the scotch is still there. There are so many things that are magnified when you're fresh out of rehab. I haven't been sober on a plane in many years. Related: I don't really like flying.

Homewood prepared me for this. A lot of people relapse on their way home. "Try to sit away from the drink cart." Check. "Have something to read." Check. "Listen to music so you don't hear glasses tinkling." Check.

I just reached into my bag and pulled out my AA and NA books. I'd asked my friends to sign them. Many wrote verses along with their signatures.

Lonzo wrote: "To my friend, Grant. Godspeed, brother. I hope your days are clean and sober. Thanks so much for your friendship. I know you'll do fine. Ha ha. Thanks for the privilege of getting me to give you your pin. Good luck and take care because I care."

I read through Bear and Silicon's messages. Dancer didn't sign it, which made me sad. It was because she left early and abruptly.

I find their words comforting.

I'm going to just sit back now and listen to the sounds of the engines.

I hear a child crying at the back of the plane.

I feel like I'm part of society again, and although starting over is difficult, it's much better than the slow, miserable death I was headed for.

My seatmate is back now, sipping on his scotch. I take a deep breath and close my eyes.

FROM "DANCER"

The first thing I did when I got to Homewood was check myself right back out again. Eleven minutes after I got there, I was gone. I ended up somehow talking myself into turning back around, but I was a reluctant patient.

I met Grant when I was outside having a cigarette. I had a pretty awful attitude around recovery and I did not want to be there. I recall saying something like, "Well, I know I'm not a doctor, but…," and he said, "Well, I am."

That kind of woke me up a bit, that there was a doctor there at rehab right alongside me.

We were both in such bad shape that we weren't allowed to leave the grounds, so we got to know each other pretty well, right off the hop.

Grant quickly became my person. I could relate to him because there were no other IV drug users there at the time. And for some reason, I trusted him. I had a real problem with authority. My IV drug use started after I was raped by a police officer. I had no trust for any sort of authority figure, including the staff at Homewood. But I trusted Grant.

He was the only person I would open up to.

I'm not sure what it was about him. He was a genuine person. He cared about people. He listened. I was used to people preaching at me. But Grant listened. He made me feel like a whole person. Not a junkie or a body part. He made me feel like I was a whole person and not just the things I had done. He used to make sure I would eat. He would take me out for coffee. He held the door open. He made me feel like I could be part of society again.

Grant helped me to remember the person I was before I got in trouble with drugs. He helped me to feel normal for the first time in a very long time. Before I met Grant, I forgot that there were good people in the world.

That being said, I didn't have a clear head at the time. And I was so used to men wanting something from me that I almost didn't trust his kindness. I was waiting to find out what he was going to want in return for being a friend to me. That never happened, but I was waiting for it.

I knew Grant was going to beat his addiction and I hated him for it. To be honest, he just seemed to want to get clean more than anyone else in the place. He was willing to put in the work and I wasn't.

I left the program early. I was asked to leave, and I agreed it wasn't the right time for me to be there. Grant almost helped me to see that. He'd said that you can't change until you're ready to change. He always believed in me, and that I would get well when the timing was right.

AFTER

My sister picked me up at the airport.

She commented on how good I looked. Like I'd been on a spa holiday. My colour was back, and I'd been more physically active over those four weeks than I had been in years. I looked like I was five years younger and felt on top of the world physically. I was very nervous about returning to the realities of PEI. There were a multitude of challenges in front of me and I knew from others' experience that there were even more than I anticipated.

On the drive home, she was telling me all these stories about my crazy behaviour leading up to my trip to rehab, and how it finally all made sense. Like the time Scarlett and I were going out and we dropped the girls off to stay with my parents. I'd left a VHS tape with them, so they could watch a Disney movie. Apparently, though, when they put the tape in the VCR, it was a homemade video from our bedroom. I had no idea it existed, and nobody told me about this before.

Everyone knew something was going on, but they were all pussyfooting around me, afraid to say anything because of how defensive I was. I went to my own doctor but was cagey with him and tried to hide the truth of what was really wrong. For example, when he checked my blood pressure I made sure to never give him the arm I was using to inject myself so he wouldn't see the fresh injection sites. He referred me to neurologists, psychiatrists, and I even had an MRI on my brain. I'm sure everyone had their suspicions about what was wrong. But I obviously was defensive so the repercussion of the accusation would be that I would retreat and not return. In truth, I think no one wanted to be the one to potentially end my career. They were all just hoping I would somehow smarten up. I, on the other hand, would lie about what was truly going on in my life. To be truthful, I was wishing they would just find a tumor or something else that would allow them some concrete reason to give me narcotics. Those were the crazy feelings I was having back then, but my time in Homewood changed that.

I was so happy to be sober, but still I was feeling lost. I didn't have a job. I wasn't a doctor anymore. My identity was completely gone.

My sister first took me to see my oldest girls. My twelve-year-old daughter ran out of her mom's house and hugged and wrapped her arms around me for at least a minute. When I saw my youngest daughter, who was two, she locked me around the neck and wouldn't let go. I was proud of what I had accomplished and the support of the people who truly loved me cemented that feeling, in a good way, inside of me. I knew I had a long road ahead of me and it was going to have to begin at home.

When I got back to my house Scarlett gave me a nod and casual embrace. Her addiction had only gotten worse while I was away. She was injecting herself right in front of me and it made me very uncomfortable. On one occasion, she broke a needle off inside her arm. After using the same syringe repeatedly, the base of the needle had undergone metal fatigue and just snapped off in her triceps muscle. This happened when we were in the car. I was forced to finish injecting her with another needle as we sat by the side of the road. This metal fatigue is much like the phenomenon that occurs with older aircraft, except in this instance the failure only leaves one with a sliver of metal in the arm and not the plunging of countless lives into the sea. Let's face it, a rocker arm breakage in the steering section of a commercial jet is a much bigger catastrophe than I was facing. But still, with my urges and demons calling at me, I felt like I was in my own hell.

I knew that it was just a matter of time.

That summer I was walking back and forth to AA meetings. It was extremely awkward to attend meetings in the beginning. I live in a small city of fewer than 50,000 people. Because I had been a doctor the local news had really started speculating on my departure. I tried not to follow the stories. I did not comment on them, under the direction of my lawyer. There was also no comment from the College of Physicians.

All that just fuelled the rumors. I was just trying to do what I was told, just like in rehab. I knew that a lot of people in AA would recognize who I was, but I also knew my disease would love for me to be uncomfortable here. At my very first meeting they asked me to read something aloud. Here I was, a physician who had read hundreds of books over my lifetime, but I stammered nervously through the reading. I almost felt like the words were getting smaller and my heart was beating so loud I couldn't hear myself speak. But I got through it, and I felt much better, almost euphoric, on my walk back home. Life was better; I was spending time with my girls, and making sure Scarlett stayed out of trouble.

I was trying to keep the house clean and trying to keep myself clean.

We were broke because my disability insurance didn't kick in for the first sixty days I was back. I had been smart enough to take out a disability plan when I graduated from medical school. To be honest I thought I might need it some day for accident or injury. But never for this. There was no money coming in. I couldn't pay Revenue Canada. I had no money left, and I had nothing to show for the money I'd spent. It had all gone to drugs or mindless extravagances I had purchased while high.

I went from having a $50,000 line of credit to having no credit. I remember breaking open all the kids' change collections and taking them into the bank. It was very humbling, but I knew I needed to do it to keep the wolves away.

Every day became about survival. The "one day at a time" philosophy I learned at Homewood was so important. I had to live each day and just live to the next one without using. I pictured my friends at Homewood and their everyday struggles. I gained strength from the fact that I was trying to be a good example for them all. I was desperately missing my team friends from rehab. The only problem with doing rehab in the middle of Canada is that I no longer had their support. I selfishly hoped they were missing me, too.

Scarlett cleaned herself up that summer. Thank God, because I was absolutely ready to walk out. I had done exactly what my AA sponsor suggested: be a good example and don't preach or lecture.

It happened August 23, 2005, just before Hurricane Katrina struck. We were glued to our television when that happened, because we'd visited New Orleans together. The hotel we'd stayed at had burnt to the ground. It was like a metaphor. The flood. The devastation. And here we were. Both clean. Both after our own storms. But right then, I felt almost as helpless as those people on their roofs with signs saying, "help me." Just like them I was still alive, but everything I had worked for was damaged. I honestly just wanted someone to rescue me. But, unfortunately, there would be no rope ladder to pull me to safety. Getting sober was one thing, but living sober together was drastically challenging. Scarlett and I were at different stages. I was all ready to start Us over again.

But she wasn't ready. She was going in a different direction than I was.

I found out in December that she had developed an interest in someone else. I confronted her and she said she wanted to work on things. But then she left the next day. I, too, slowly figured out the things didn't include me. I didn't blame her at all. I had been a less-than-perfect partner.

I started to fall apart. I was going to meetings every day to keep myself clean. It seemed as if my choices were becoming frayed. It is extremely difficult to follow and believe in something that isn't tangible.

The irony is that currently we all do that. Advances in technology have changed the way we learn, communicate, and ultimately think. There is no human face behind the directions we follow every day. It seems to be easy for people to follow faceless directions, but it was hard for me. I shoved my strong connection with my higher power aside basically because of pride, disappointment, and frustration. I was shifting back to rudimentary thinking, and it would be a harsh lesson.

On Christmas Day, I was feeling especially low. I remember someone telling me one time about how it helps to go out and throw eggs off a cliff, just to watch them smash. So, I rounded up some hoodlums from early recovery and while everyone else was celebrating, we were out throwing eggs at buildings. Me, a forty-year-old doctor.

When I got home, I looked at my sad, bent Christmas

tree sitting in the empty dining room. My friends had forced me to put it up. Where had things gone so desperately wrong? I had been doing so well and now I was acting like an out-of-control teenager. But I could not seem to reach that glimpse of hope that I had had before. I could almost feel myself being pulled in a direction that scared me, and as much as I tried to fight it I felt that anything short of institutionalization wasn't going to stop it. But that was impossible now—at least, that is what I thought. So many people were counting on me and watching me.

Later that week, the same crew of us decided to go to Moncton for a road trip. We had fun and this became our thing: to hit the road and just get off PEI. There is something to being off the Island. It feels like you aren't the same person and that can be dangerous.

On one of these trips, a couple of guys decided they were going to drink. They had maybe two-and-a-half years of sobriety between them. Me at just six months. But I drank, too. I drank twenty-five double tequilas that night in a contest at the bar. I ended up falling and hurting myself. It was messy. But I felt like I was part of a group again. I was trying to replace that empty feeling that Scarlett was leaving in my core.

And I'd told myself that drinking was okay. If I didn't go back to narcotics it would be okay. But I was just binging like I had in Lunenburg.

As January went on, I became more and more depressed. My brother's birthday was coming up on January 21.

One of my buddies from recovery suggested that he and I go to Moncton. We were going to go without the rest of the group, and our plan was to get drunk.

We stopped at the liquor store on the way. I felt like a kid in a candy store. An addict in recovery (because that's what I was—I'd just been focusing on the drugs during rehab instead of the booze) planning to drink again? Wow. I was so excited I didn't know what to pick. I felt like someone who had been on a strict diet and suddenly I could eat all the things I love. I bought a pint of fireball and a huge bottle of the highest percentage wine I could find.

We drank the Fireball whiskey as we drove. I threw my AA book into the back of the van defiantly. I distinctly remember playing the song "Wake Me Up When September Ends" by Green Day. I still get visions of these moments every time I hear that song.

When we got to Moncton, we parked the car at a parkade. We called a cab from there to take us to a club. I wasn't allowed to have the alcohol in the cab, obviously, so I chugged the litre-and-a-half of wine.

We ended up at a strip club and I didn't want to hang around there. I never liked strip clubs. And there was talk of going back to the hotel rooms with some of the girls. I was in no shape emotionally to handle that situation. So, apparently, I took off.

And I woke up in a jail cell. Deep down inside I'd been wishing for that feeling of the plastic covering on my face, but it was a bare metal bed. No pillow and no blanket.

An RCMP officer asked me if I remembered what had happened the night before.

I couldn't tell him anything. I'd blacked out.

Apparently, I had been walking around outside in minus-twenty-degree temperatures with no coat on. I do remember something about being booked into the cell, but the rest is just not there.

My buddy must have taken my keys from my coat, which I'd left behind at the bar, and somehow made it to the parkade. He took my car for a spin around a subdivision doing sixty miles per hour. I can just imagine that he had been looking for me in a drunken haze.

He hit a large granite boulder. The van ran over it, ripping the gas tank and everything went ablaze. When they told me, I was so shocked that I was in a daze.

The RCMP officer was kind enough to drive me to the hospital. He took ten dollars out of his own wallet and gave it to me because he knew I hadn't eaten that day. I have thought of him since; he never did give me his name.

I was there when the doctors told my friend he would never walk again, and his pregnant girlfriend said that she didn't know whether to hug me or hit me. I really knew I wasn't responsible, but it still made me feel like shit. What the hell was going on with my life? I had a long time to think about it in the cafeteria of that hospital, waiting the five hours for my friends from PEI to come and get me. My emotions were driving my actions and I had to sort them out. I am such an idiot, I said to myself. I have been given a second chance and I am totally blowing it. Meanwhile, my disease is screaming that next time I drink it will be different. It will be fun and maybe I will meet someone amazing. But reality was sinking in. This was a struggle between devotion to my sickness and to other human beings.

I think that all it came down to was love. I know that I loved Beth; I think that I loved Scarlett's dark side; and sure as hell I somehow loved Dancer. But I think my biggest love was not being myself. Since the Golden Boy was gone I didn't know who I was anymore, and that intense fear made me drink. I would have to use extreme action to take myself back to the centre of reality: the reality being that life is what it is and I was going to have to live every second of it fully aware. I would have to learn to love myself to accomplish this daunting task. I needed someone's advice on how to achieve this peace. I was going down a rabbit hole.

I remembered this older man I saw at AA and sought out his help. I remembered travelling to his trailer and him telling me that Scarlett was like a slippery football: the more I held on to her the more like she would slip away. This was simple, I could understand this.

He also told me to go back through the twelve steps and to focus on Step Four. Follow the simple instructions in the book of AA.

Step Four is: Write down your resentments and things you're resentful about.

- I resented my ex-wife for taking all my money. But I'd cheated on her.

- I resented Beth for leaving me. But I was the one who'd changed.
- I resented Scarlett for cheating on me. But I'd willingly gotten involved with a drug addict.
- I resented the College of Physicians for getting rid of me. But I'd been doing drugs.
- I resented my brother for dying.

Every one of those resentments...they were all my fault. Except for Guy. I was carrying so much guilt. He never would have wanted this for me. He was four years older than me, so throughout my life he had always protected me. Although very different from me, he was brilliant in various ways. His IQ was a bit higher than mine, but it was more geared to the technical realms. He was the only member of my family who really supported me through my first divorce, and I would talk to him by phone almost every day through that crisis. He was acting like my big brother again, but there had been years of turmoil before that point.

I guess all this changed when, in in his early twenties, he developed bipolar disorder and the roles reversed. They not only altered for me but my entire family. It was difficult adjustment because he was so intelligent and driven. I remember him as a kid pretending to be a radio announcer and he would stay up late in our bedroom, talking on the CB radio. He learned Morse code and spoke to people throughout the world. He ended up becoming a radio announcer in his late teens. He was very successful in his profession, especially because of his uncanny grasp of technical equipment.

It was when I was in medical school that his unsettling behaviour began. He would spend money in extravagant amounts and would develop grandiose, unrealistic plans. He was so good at his job and was so smart that it was hard to decipher brilliance from mental illness, but in reality it was a combination of both.

He was, however, one of my hugest supporters in those dark days of family and social isolation. Besides my friend Donald, he was the one person I could tell most things to. One thing we didn't share with each other, unfortunately, was our struggles with opioids. I was too proud to tell him, and I suspect the same applied to him. I had become the arrogant little brother just because I helped him out financially several times. I remember sitting on my parents' front steps on one occasion and him showing me the new cowboy boots he'd bought. I was resentful that he could buy these when he owed me money, so instead of being supportive and complimentary, I told him a joke that Dr. Barry Ling had told me that day. "What do hemorrhoids and cowboy boots have in common? Sooner or later every asshole has them." I will never forget the look on his face and if I could take five sentences back over my lifetime this would be one. I knew I really hurt his feelings, and, furthermore, he had come to respect my opinion so what I had said was very wounding. There was a divide that was developing between us. I was struggling that summer with stopping narcotics, without any outside help. He was also struggling, but I think he was too proud or too ashamed to ask his brother for help, especially when the brother was acting like a total dick.

When I look back on it, his behaviour over the last few months of his life was more of someone physically dependent on narcotics rather than an addict. He seemed to be taking too many sometimes, but all in all he was quite functional. He was an avid goose hunter and the day he died was the day before the season opened. I am sure he was just trying to get out of withdrawal so he could get all his gear ready for an early morning start the next day. I knew it wasn't my fault because I didn't know any better, but I could have been more helpful at the time. I could have explained the situation to a colleague and asked them to see him. In AA there is an expression: "If they knew better they would do better" and certainly that applied to me. I had to go through my own hell to feel the sense of desperation he must have been feeling that day. Coupled with his bipolar illness and his feelings of withdrawal, it created a perfect storm for catastrophe.

I wrote him a letter and I took it to his grave. I read it to him and then I burned it. I looked at the dog sculpture that is part of his gravestone. He loved dogs, especially Labrador retrievers. He had such a secret side to his life. I may never understand him, but that is okay. I loved him and I have forgiven both of us for our mistakes.

I freed myself from the guilt I'd been carrying. And

I was done with drinking and trying to hide or blur how I felt. I was going to be truthful and real. I couldn't promise that it would last forever, but I knew it was going to last at least that day. I kept stringing those days together.

I stayed clean for the rest of that winter, attending meetings. Staying clean took all my energy. I didn't focus on much else. But life was certainly interesting. I remember on one occasion after attending an AA meeting I was standing with a group of guys waiting to order a coffee at the Tim Horton's on Kent Street. Some guy in the group struck up a conversation and then told a story about the whole incident that had unfolded in Moncton. That I had been the drunk driver and that someone else had ended up paralyzed. The truth was that had it not been for a father and daughter team pulling him from the burning vehicle he could not have gotten out himself and he would not be alive. I just listened to his banter and then very calmly, after hearing my name mentioned a third time, said, "I am Grant Matheson and we should make sure we have our facts straight before we gossip." I exited through the two sets of glass doors, not really waiting to see his reaction. My friend who I will call Stick followed me. He was handsome and thin, and had about four years of sobriety at the time, and was one of the two who had come to pick me up in Moncton that fateful day. He said something I will never forget: "Grant, people love talking about your situation because it makes them feel better about themselves. Don't take it the wrong way, buddy, everyone is hoping you make it in the end. But your spills make them feel better about their own situations."

Spills was an interesting choice of words. I always hated spills because there was obviously less in the glass. The irony again was that less in the glass would be better for me. I could only grow to appreciate how full my glass of life was, but also accept and appreciate the spills. I just had to go on with my own life one day at a time and try to put Scarlett and that life behind me. I met a woman in March and we started a low-stress relationship. She was a social drinker but that didn't bother me, and things were good. She was funny, energetic, loyal, and most of all she didn't judge me. I was content.

That summer I took a labour job with a handyman to help pass the time. I was working for a man in AA who couldn't drive his truck because his license had been revoked. He needed me to drive, and to help him. I needed some money, although the guy was so honest he hardly made any money himself. But that didn't matter: I felt productive and was staying sober. I had an amazing summer. We laughed about the silliest things. It reminded me of having a summer job as a teen. Not much money but so much fun. I so appreciated his company and I almost felt like I was back in rehab again.

In 2007, I started back to work as a locum doctor. I started out working about twenty hours a week. It felt good going back to work, and things started to feel normal. It was strange using my signature again. It was something I used to do hundreds of times a day before rehab, and I had barely needed it since then.

That fall I started working my own clinic again. The Murphy's Pharmacy group was excellent to me. They gave me a space to set up my office and helped me hire staff that would protect me. After all, I knew I was a people pleaser so I needed support staff that would have my back—and they did.

The winter ticked along without incident. News of my drug addiction had circulated throughout the community and my patients were very understanding. Everyone was supportive and just seemed happy that they hadn't lost another doctor.

The other doctors, however, weren't all one hundred per cent happy with me. I had been guilty of using my relationship with some of them to sign prescriptions that were questionable in hindsight. They had put their careers on the line for me, and I still feel guilty about that to this day. Others just had problems with trusting me.

In April 2008, I received word that I was being charged with committing fraud under $5,000, for writing prescriptions that were being partially diverted to me. These incidents all happened prior to my admission to Homewood.

The man who had been supplying me with drugs heard that I'd returned to work. I now understand his motivation for reporting me, but at the time I felt betrayed.

I was taken to the police station and read the charges. Everything that I was being charged with was true. My head subconsciously nodded yes, as the detective read the charges to me. As I left the building with my lawyer I felt totally defeated.

Not only was this man the attorney for the Canadian Medical Protective Association or CMPA (and therefore every physician in PEI), but he was one of my best friends and had been the best man at my wedding to Beth. He witnessed the union of this ideal love and then its unravelling. Then he watched me rise again from the burning ashes of a controversial disease, only to be shot down by my own prior transgressions. He is one of the most brilliant minds I know—not only for his legal skills but for his intuitive capacity. So, I trusted him completely. He helped me through many a College interrogation, many I can barely recall. The most amazing thing about him is that he could walk that line between friendship and client. He never made me feel judged or that I couldn't tell him anything. Quite the opposite: the only person in the world that I professionally trusted was Jim Gormley, QC.

He encouraged me to take responsibility for my actions. This also happened to be the best legal advice. But he would always make sure that I was treated fairly in both the justice and my professional system. His first advice to me after the charges were laid against me was crucial in my journey, not only from a legal perspective, but from a recovery standpoint. He recommended and set up an appointment to go back and see the doctor who first confronted me at Homewood, Dr. Graeme Cunningham.

He was the very doctor who stopped my addiction circus act of juggling multiple plates—or, rather, lies.

I was afraid. But my gut feeling, as was his, that this was the right thing for me to do under the circumstances. He arranged for me to see him on Tuesday, the same day as the Caduceus meeting. That way I would get the opinion of health professionals who may have faced similar circumstances. I remember that it was around April 20, 2008. It was hot but I rented a little air-conditioned Volvo. It was liberating to be off PEI, enjoying the nicer weather, not scared for me and my family, or that the media were going to show up outside my house. I know I am not that popular, but PEI is a small place.

Sure enough, I got to see Dr. Cunningham himself. I was seeing him on different terms now: I had been sober for more than two years, working without a narcotic license, and doing biweekly urine tests. I explained the situation, as did Jim Gormley. I knew the obstacles. So did Jim. He intentionally chose the same physician whom the College of Physicians and Surgeons had chosen in 2005: the physician who first broke through my denial and offered the opinion that I was sick and addicted. These opinions were used to suspend me.

Now Dr. Cunningham was seeing me under a different set of circumstances and, for the record, his recommendations this time were ignored. I'm certain that the College's minds were already made up and that was, honestly, okay with me. I wanted to walk with my head high again. Like I did when my Dad asked me at age ten to sit in the front row and tape the church service. I would make sure I hit those tape and play buttons just at the right time. I would be all dressed up in that three-piece itchy woollen suit. I would be so filled with essence of the hymns, the stained glass, and the feelings that were like a warm wave coming over me. I felt that spirituality but didn't know how to grasp it.

But right then I just wanted to know how to get out of this fucking situation. For me, my kids, and my patients and staff. I was so tired of the word narcotic; its utterance almost made me sick. Right then, I needed the support of people who understood and embraced me, to be advised by colleagues who had been in similar situations. I needed to hear what the Caduceus group of experience health professionals had to say, and just get home and hug my kids.

The group decision was unanimous: plead guilty and see what happens. No matter if the source has a vengeful or even retaliatory purpose.

I knew I couldn't just run away. I had to face the music.

I went back home and kept on working. The issue didn't go to court until December. I pled guilty and tearfully apologized for my behaviour. How could I expect to get away with something I myself would have condemned only years before? The judge sentenced me a conditional discharge. I would be on probation for two years. During that time, I would have to have random drug tests and speak to several groups about the dangers of prescription drug use.

The College was looking for a suspension of three-and-a-half years. We got a stay from the judge, and the Supreme Court of PEI overturned the decision in the summer of that same year. I didn't get suspended.

I continued to work. I exercised daily, I attended twelve-step meetings regularly, I tried to stay connected to a higher power every day. If I did that, everything was fine.

Unfortunately, five years later, I crumbled again because I stopped doing all those things. I was too busy trying to find my next girlfriend to listen to my higher power. I didn't return to drugs, but I did end up addicted again: this time to alcohol. Fortunately, my family and friends arranged an intervention.

It was Labour Day of 2012. I couldn't figure out why my oldest daughters just didn't seem to want to leave that day. But suddenly I found myself surrounded by most of the people I loved, along with a facilitator who was a former priest and who had been sober for twenty-five years. I must admit I was half-buzzed at the time, but the reality of the situation came crashing down on me when my oldest daughters read letters to me that they had prepared. I saw that Jim Gormley was present so I knew the situation was serious. I realized I needed help again, and the next day I was on a flight back to Homewood accompanied by my sister.

At least for this second trip to Homewood I had her. She was gracious enough to let me drink the whole trip. I had been drinking around the clock for the week leading up to that point, so it was probably the best decision. My sister doesn't drink at all, so this was, I'm sure, a stretch for her. Alcohol withdrawal can cause severe prolonged deadly seizures and that was the last thing she wanted to happen to me during the flight.

When I checked into Homewood I found out that the psychiatrist that I had been so mad at after my brother's death was behind my most recent referral. We had become very close over the years and I came to realize that he had no idea how much distress my brother was in that fateful day, or he would have made time for him. Deep down inside I knew a phone call from me would have likely helped, but I had to let that go.

There were a lot of people behind getting me help this time. I felt like a horse that fell through the ice and couldn't understand that people were trying to bring him to safety. I felt like somehow people were attacking me and I would try to fight them off. But that didn't matter now because I was here safely. There was a familiar smell of hand sanitizer and the familiar wristband. I can barely remember entering the building, just walking into my room, really.

They urine-tested me to be sure they were treating just pure alcohol withdrawal, which of course I knew they were. But active addicts and alcoholics tend to be sparse with the truth. They packed my clothes away and the same physician who attended to me during my first admission was there. I was given an injection of thiamine and 60mg of Valium to stop the shaking that was not only physically apparent but also emotionally obvious. Narcotic withdrawal feels more miserable, but alcohol withdrawal can be deadly. But I knew I was in a safe place.

As I lay on my bed I kept saying to myself: how did I end up here again? I was so angry with the fact that I had let this disease slip in the back door. I was thankful that I was safe and I quickly grasped that I could settle into the routine that I knew would restore me to health again. I could feel the plastic pillow covering below my pillowcase. It was strange, but as upset as I was at the time I was looking forward to the experience. I had stopped looking at rehab as a punishment a long time ago. It was more of a tune-up for those who are inclined to drift down the path of chemical indulgence. I had flashbacks of my previous time here. It would surely be a different experience, but that is all part of the journey, and the best way to approach it is with appreciation and excitement. As I faded off to sleep I knew when I woke up I would take on this challenge by just letting go and trusting the process. All the right people will be put in my path as they had before. I felt that glimmer of faith again. Like the feeling of that warm facecloth my mother would put on my forehead when I was sick.

AFTER AFTER

You need a fortress around you to keep that abusive lover from calling you back.

It's easy to forget how bad it is. To romance the good times.

Addiction is a lifelong disease.

I would like to say that I won't go back there, but that would be naïve. I can say that I work on maintaining my sobriety every single day.

I know what it means to lose everything, and I don't have any interest in doing that again. After my children, my sobriety is the most important thing in the world to me. And I have realized that abusing substances will destroy my life. With narcotics, it will do it quickly, and with alcohol, it will do it more slowly and insidiously. It is much like boarding an extravagant cruise on a sinking ship. But the gash in the hull depends totally on the substance and is totally out of my control.

As I ponder the affliction that is now certainly my label, I can't help but wonder how I got here. Many parts of medicine have tried to treat the addict but have failed. Even more have inadvertently been a catalyst to the condition, only to throw their hands up in despair when the patient fails to respond rationally. The problem is that addiction, in my opinion, is a disease of irrational thinking that is first precipitated by a crisis in a person's life. It is then fuelled by an emotionally numbing agent. Once the cascade of mental unfitness has been fuelled by an accelerating agent, the point of no return can be swift and merciless. No caregiver would do this intentionally: give someone destructive advice. It would be like advising someone who was cold to go home and sit by a warm fire, not realizing they had a gas leak in their house; the counsellor in this instance had no idea of the person's separate crisis or imminent threat.

If it was me *giving* the advice I would likely be defensive, and, frankly, arrogant; how could I have known all the circumstances? There would of course be no intent because the prescription was given without knowledge of the underlying situation. And the accepter of the prescription might not realize that they are in a fragile mental or situational state. I, myself, had no idea how impacted I was by the shame I felt for my brother's death.

Society has placed this condition in the wrong category for too long. No one intentionally causes this, it is a combination of circumstances. The more important thing is that we remove the negative label from the condition. Who would seek help for any medical condition or mental fragility, if it met with public scrutiny, bias, and job loss? I can say this from my own experience that this is a condition, much like a mental illness, that one tends to not admit publicly. Especially when it arises and is seen as a weakness or a relapse or a slip. People who struggle with other terminal illnesses are treated more graciously. There are no cakes for the addict who uses again, no flowers for the alcoholic who met a life crisis and got drunk.

Let's just all be less judgmental of each other and be part of the solution for this epidemic. Judging addicts is not only part of their disease, but is exactly how the disease wants you to look at them. I know that until I had gone through this experience I would have never even entertained such ideas. But from one golden boy to another, how about we just cut everyone a bit of slack? Everyone else is not as perfect as we are right now.

Before I finished writing this book, I went on a trip to Vancouver with my youngest daughter for a soccer tournament. I wanted to take a drive around some of the most drug-infested streets in the city. The other soccer dads asked me if I was crazy. Why would I want to go somewhere so dangerous?

I explained that these were my people. I was one of them. Addicts are only dangerous if you take away their access. These people are sick, not bad.

I attended a meeting while I was there. I wanted to see for myself if this disease has any geographic differences. It doesn't. I have attended meetings in the fancy suburbs of Orlando, Florida, and the backstreets of Vancouver. The stories are very different but the outcomes all the same. Wreckage and carnage to varying degrees, but the ship always eventually sinks. I still attend meetings wherever I go, because they help me. Sharing my story helps me.

As I was writing this I remembered an intervention that I missed. It was in the fall of 2004, by a pharmacist who was in the program. He pulled up beside my vehicle at the edge of a mall parking lot. I had just tried to obtain quantities of injectable narcotics that I had claimed were for my Botox and cosmetic facial filler clients in my clinics. He asked me to get into his vehicle and he proceeded to ask me if anyone was forcing me or putting me up to this. He was basically giving me a way out and I was in such denial or was too scared to admit what I was doing. He said that he could help me if that was the case, but I refused to admit that there was an issue. I will never know if he could have helped.

I am sure that there are many such instances in a person's life where help is offered but we think we can handle it ourselves. This may be true for a lot of things, but with narcotic addiction our foe is a fiery dragon that can't be slain alone. If I had broken down and told that pharmacist the truth, perhaps things would have been different. But I would not have had the experiences I've had and I most certainly would not have had the opportunity to speak up about this issue. Is that a silver lining?

Another thing I did while I was writing this book? I took a trip to Homewood again. I wanted to see it again through sober eyes. I walked around the grounds and remembered. I took pictures of the places that meant the most to me, areas where I felt I had my deepest conversations and felt my deepest connections.

I owe a lot to that place, and to the people I met there.

One of the doctors who helped me relapsed. At first, I felt sorry for him, but then I realized that, like me, we can learn from these experiences, if we survive them, and we become better humans. It is sort of like a great relationship: sometimes an interruption in what seems like plodding makes one appreciate just how good life is.

THANKS

The people around me have been affected by my experience. My children have all been amazing and I am very proud of each of them. My parents have really changed the most. Our relationship wasn't the best after my first divorce, but I have watched their faith grow through this process. They have ended up being the ones I can count on the most, and they don't preach at me anymore but are this haven of sanity that is always there for me. I don't feel that pressure from them to be perfect anymore. I can be totally honest with them and I don't feel judged.

Something that still amazes me is that all the people in my extended family still love me and me them. My first ex-wife, with whom I am still dear friends, was part of the group that gathered for my intervention. Beth has forgiven me for developing a relationship with Scarlett and has become a tremendous support for me. We are still very close and would do anything for each other. I have met a woman who may become my wife; her understanding and support are crucial.

Several of the people I met along my journey aren't with us anymore. I am thankful every single day that I am. Dancer is finally sober—more than a year now. She and I keep in touch; there will always be a place in my heart for her. Bear has been sober since his stay at Homewoood. Danger had some struggles early on, but now she has a new baby and looks as gorgeous and dangerous as ever. I have lost track of Jock, Cleveland, and Silicon. Silicon, I often wonder about you, so if you are out there, buddy, I would truly love to hear from you.

I would not be where I am today without the true friendship of Jim Gormley and Donne Buell. The thing that distinguishes these two from others is that neither of them suffered from the same disease as me, yet both could somehow get me to open up to them without judging me for my outlandish behaviour. One of the reasons addicts seek out other recovering addicts for help is this fear of being judged or being labelled as mentally unstable. Most of my behaviour when I was using was very irrational, but these individuals had the ability to absorb the chaos I would divulge, and make it seem human.

Life has a funny way of working out. The seasons will come and go, just like our problems. The one thing that I have learned from this experience is that life is really about acceptance and faith. Existence is like a continuous movie and we must accept the roles that are given to us daily.

I have been humbled by this ordeal. I have much less

control over my daily fate than I ever would have imagined. It is true that I can manage by controlling my surroundings, but then there is also what goes on inside of us, in our bodies and minds. These we can only influence by proper management. Believing that things will always turn out okay allows us to take the all-important deep breath. How can we enjoy life if we are always looking over our shoulder? I also believe in being fully aware of our surroundings and not going through life heedlessly.

I have also learned—the hard way—that fretting and self-loathing are the opposite of life. It is almost impossible to grow when these emotions become dominant. If we believe that our experiences are all part of a greater purpose, then they become more bearable. We all should find our own divine power and not be judging each other. We are not as different as we had reckoned. Over the decades the scope of our differences has just changed, but we are basically the same. We are all in this together, and, to be honest, it would be difficult to envision life differently. Don't let others or your disease determine who you are.

When I was at Homewood I thought about whether I might like to work there one day. I think I would. But I'm not sure yet what my future holds.

For now, I still live in Prince Edward Island. My eldest daughters are in their twenties. My youngest is in junior high school. She keeps me on her toes with her athletics schedule. I am grateful that my daughters have forgiven me.

I haven't worked since my second stay at Homewood and I don't suspect I'll ever work as a doctor in PEI again. Right now, that is my own choice. To clear the air of all the speculation I haven't taken a narcotic since that airport bathroom incident more than twelve years ago.

My hope is that someday I may be given the opportunity to work with medical students and other health professionals to open some eyes to the dangers of prescribing opioids and self-medicating.

I hope this book will change your perspective about addicts. Addicts are sick. They are not bad. For me? It started completely innocently. It started with a cough. If it can happen to a respected physician, addiction can happen to anyone.

I am no longer a doctor. I am no longer the golden boy.

I am just Grant.

And I am no different than you.